Umberto's PASTA BOOK

by Umberto Menghi

DAVID ROBINSON, PUBLISHER

FOR WHITECAP BOOKS

copyright © 1985 Umberto Menghi, Ron Lammie and Patrizio Sacchetto

A David Robinson Book

Whitecap Books
1086 West 3rd Street
North Vancouver
British Columbia V7P 3J6
Canada

This book was typeset by Hemlock Printers,
designed by David Robinson, and printed in Canada
by Hemlock Printers for David Robinson, Publisher.

The text and cover photographs were taken by
Derik Murray. Food preparation by John Bishop.

First printing: February 1985

Canadian Cataloguing in Publication Data

Menghi, Umberto, 1946 –
   Umberto's pasta book

   Includes index.
   ISBN 0-920620-62-0

   1. Cookery (Macaroni) I. Title.
   TX809.M17M45 1984   641.8'22   C84-091462-8

Table of Contents

Introduction / 5

Introduction

This book comes to you from a man who knows pasta well. Umberto Menghi grew up in Italy, where pasta is a way of life. Pasta has always been on the menu of Umberto's restaurants in North America. Umberto has written about pasta in his previous cookbook, *The Umberto Menghi Cookbook*; he has talked about it on his syndicated TV show, "The Elegant Appetite"; and, now, through Umbertino's, his eat-in, take-out, home delivery pasta emporiums, Umberto is taking pasta to the streets.

Umberto's Pasta Book is the latest up-to-the-minute pasta book. There is something for everyone in *Umberto's Pasta Book*. In it, you will find all your traditional favourite recipes (recipes for Spaghetti Amatriciana, Linguine alle Vongole, Tortellini alla Panna, etc.), plus recipes for the new pasta, *pasta nuova*, where the sauces tend to be light and diet-conscious, made with consommés, vegetable purées and fresh herbs; and where clean, distinct tastes, colour and visual presentation are of the utmost importance.

Umberto's Pasta Book is an A to Z pasta book—a guide to 21 different noodles, from agnolotti to ziti; and to the making of 41 different kinds of pasta, from the standard egg noodle pasta, through herb, spinach and beet pasta, to black squid ink pasta. The book is organized by the noodle, rather than by the sauce. All the recipes in the book are for 1 lb./500 g of pasta, which serves 4 people as a main course, or 6 people in appetizer portions. If you are serving 2 people, use 1/2 lb./250 g of pasta and cut the recipes for sauce in half.

The recipes in this book have been culled from the menus of Umberto's four superb restaurants in Vancouver (Umberto's, Il Giardino di Umberto, La Cantina di Umberto, Umberto al Porto), his two restaurants in Seattle (Umberto's and La Galleria di Umberto), his restaurant in San Francisco (Umberto's) and his restaurant at Whistler Mountain Ski Village (Il Caminetto di Umberto); and they have been created by the *maestro* himself from his wide knowledge of food. "Attitudes to food have changed a lot in recent years," Umberto says. "People are eating less meat and more fresh produce." Pasta is a perfect vehicle for these changing attitudes towards food. Pasta, which was once thought of as only Macaroni and Cheese or Spaghetti and Meatballs, is now a food of ultimate sophistication. It has infinite variety and it can be elegantly served on any occasion.

As far as the facts are concerned, pasta is made from a simple combination of flour and eggs. It is a carbohydrate food, high in protein and low in fat (not counting the sauce, which could be high in protein and low in fat—and low in calories); and it contains vitamins and iron. Pasta is a healthy food. It is good for you. Statistical evidence shows that carbohydrate foods are more *satisfying* to people than other types of food; and, historically, people have evolved on a diet of grain. Not only is pasta nutritious—it is easy to digest. Ounce for ounce, pasta has *less* calories and cholesterol than a steak! If you are diet-conscious, the only thing you have to watch with pasta is the sauce—and overeating! Pasta is so *good,* it's hard to stop eating it!

Pasta is as old as the centuries and as new as today. When questioned as to whether or not the pasta trend has peaked, Umberto just laughs. "Pasta is the longest on-going trend in the history of food," he says, and the "food of the future," he has always maintained. Pasta is probably the most democratic food in the world. It is inexpensive, straightforward and easy-to-prepare. You can do so much with pasta! Pasta comes in all sorts of shapes and sizes—in many more than the 21 different varieties in this book— and you can be quite inventive with it. In this book, you can mix and match sauces with different kinds of noodles—or try any of the coloured pastas with the recipes for sauces. The basic rule of thumb is that flat, broad noodles, or tubular noodles, go with assertive, chunky sauces; and that thinner, finer noodles go with finer, more delicate sauces, the cream or consommé or vegetable purée sauces—sauces that coat the noodle—but use your intuition and go with what looks good and feels right to you.

Be imaginative with pasta! Have fun with it and *enjoy* what you are doing. Pasta should be cooked "con amore," Umberto says—"with love." And then he adds: "RECORDATI, AL DENTE!" "REMEMBER, FIRM TO THE BITE!"

Vancouver, B.C.
February, 1985

How to Make Pasta

How to Make Pasta—pasta is a simple combination of flour and eggs.

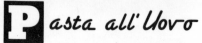# Pasta all' Uovo

Homemade Egg Noodle Pasta

For approx. 1 lb./500 g fresh pasta

Serves 4-6

1 cup/250 mL & 2 tbsp./25 mL all-purpose flour
1 cup/250 mL & 2 tbsp./25 mL semolina flour
3 eggs
1/2 tsp./2 mL salt

Part One: Making the Dough

Put flour in a mound on a clean, flat work surface. Make a well in the centre of the mound of flour and break eggs into the well. Add salt to eggs, and using a fork or a small wire whisk, gently beat eggs until eggs and salt are mixed together, then gradually incorporate flour from all sides of the mound into the egg mixture until a thick paste forms. Once a paste forms, mix in the rest of the flour using your hands. Work quickly until the dough forms a ball. If the dough is sticky or moist, add a bit more flour until the dough stops sticking to your hands. Place dough under a ceramic bowl for 30 minutes. Clean work area thoroughly, leaving no crumbs of dough on the work surface. Wash your hands, removing all traces of dough, then dry your hands well.

Part Two: Kneading and Rolling the Dough

Method One: Kneading and Rolling the Dough by Hand

Lightly flour your hands and the work surface. Begin kneading the dough by slightly flattening the ball of dough and folding it in half towards you. Knead the dough away from you with the heel of your hand, then fold it over towards you. Repeat this process, turning the dough around in a circle as you knead it for about 10 minutes until it is smooth and elastic. (If you are doubling the recipe or using more than 2 eggs, divide the dough in half at this point and put one-half of the dough under the ceramic bowl while you work on the other half of the dough.) Lightly flour the work surface once again and lightly flour a rolling pin. Slightly flatten the ball of dough once again and begin to roll away from you to open the ball out. After each roll, rotate the dough so that it stays circular. Repeat this process until the dough is about 1/8 inch/.25 cm thick. In order to get the pasta paper thin, a different method of rolling must be used from now on. Lightly flour the work surface and the rolling pin once again. Curl the far end of the dough around the rolling pin and roll towards you, stopping about one-quarter of the way into the dough. Slide your hands along the dough under the rolling pin, gently stretching it to either side away from the centre at the same time as you roll the dough backwards and forwards. Repeat this process, rolling up a little more of the dough each time until the entire sheet of dough has been rolled up and stretched. When the entire sheet of dough has been rolled up on the rolling pin, lift the dough and turn it about 45° before unrolling it. This way, you will start stretching and rolling a new area of the sheet of dough. Repeat this stretching and rolling process until the sheet of pasta is paper thin. Do not roll any longer than 10 minutes as the sheet of pasta will dry out. For agnolotti, the pasta must be cut, stuffed and cooked right away. It cannot be left to dry. The pasta must be moist so that it will adhere and keep the stuffing in. For cannelloni, fettuccine, lasagna or pappardelle, lay a clean, dry towel on a work surface and lay the dough on the towel, allowing one-third of it to hang over the edge of the work surface. Let dough dry for 30 minutes, turning

8

it over 2-3 times. The pasta is ready to cut when it is dry to the touch. Do not let the pasta dry too much as it will be impossible to handle. To cut, put dough on a cutting board. Use a sharp knife or a serrated dough cutter. For agnolotti and cannelloni, cut into 4 inch/10 cm squares. For fettuccine or pappardelle, fold dough in a flat roll 3 inches/8 cm wide and cut across dough to the appropriate thickness, then gently unfold. For lasagna noodles, cut into 5 x 3 inch/12.5 x 8 cm pieces for easier handling and let noodles dry an extra 10 minutes. Once homemade pasta is completely dry, it can be stored in a large glass jar, but you will probably want to eat it fresh. If you are not using the stuffed pasta right away, it must be refrigerated or frozen. Only flat noodles can be rolled by hand.

Method Two: Kneading Dough by Hand and Rolling It Through a Pasta Machine

Lightly flour your hands and the work surface. Begin kneading the dough by slightly flattening the ball of dough and folding it in half towards you. Knead the dough away from you with the heel of your hand, then fold it over towards you. Repeat this process, turning the dough around in a circle as you knead it for 3-4 minutes. Divide the dough into balls the size of oranges. Work on one ball of dough at a time, leaving the others under a ceramic bowl. Put pasta machine rollers at the widest setting. Slightly flatten one ball of dough and flour it lightly. Feed dough through the pasta machine 5-6 times with the rollers set at the widest setting. Let dough fold onto itself as it comes through the rollers. If the dough sticks, dust it with flour. Adjust rollers to the next thinnest setting and feed the dough through the pasta machine 1 time. Do not let dough fold onto itself this time. Repeat, adjusting the rollers to the next thinnest and the next thinnest setting. Do not let dough fold onto itself and, if it sticks, dust with flour. If the dough gets too long to handle, cut in half and process one-half at a time. Repeat until the dough has been through the rollers at all the settings. Lay dough between two clean cloths. Repeat for each ball of dough. If you are making stuffed pasta, proceed with cutting, stuffing and cooking the pasta right away. Stuffing should be ready at this time. If you are not making stuffed pasta, let the pasta dry for 10 minutes. Cut by hand or insert cutting blades into your machine. To cut by hand, see instructions above. If cutting by machine, insert appropriate blade into machine and feed dough through the machine one last time. Store pasta in glass jars or eat it fresh.

To make coloured pasta, consult the following chart. We have listed 40 different kinds of pasta that you can make by adding ingredients with the flour and eggs when you're making the pasta. For specific recipes for many of these different coloured pastas, look under the following noodles in this book: fettuccine, lasagna, rigatoni and rotini. Use 2 cups/500 mL flour: a mixture of 1 cup/250 mL all-purpose flour and 1 cup/250 mL semolina flour. Choose whatever ingredient you wish to add to the pasta, process as indicated in the chart, and blend with the eggs and salt when you are adding them to the well of flour (follow instructions for making Homemade Egg Noodle Pasta). The trick is to purée or finely chop (for fruit, vegetables or herbs) whatever ingredient you're adding until it is *very fine*.

Kind of Pasta	Combination of Flour		Add (blend with)	Number of Large Eggs
	1 cup/250 mL all-purpose flour	1 cup/250 mL semolina flour		
Whole Wheat	1 cup/250 mL all-purpose flour	1 cup/250 mL whole wheat		4
Rye	1 cup/250 mL all-purpose flour	1 cup/250 mL rye flour		4-5
Four Grain	1/2 cup/125 mL all-purpose flour	1/2 cup/125 mL semolina 1/2 cup/125 mL whole wheat 1/2 cup/125 mL bran		4-5
Herbed	1 cup/250 mL all-purpose flour	1 cup/250 mL semolina flour	1/4 cup/50 mL mixture of fresh herbs, very finely chopped (basil, oregano, rosemary, sage, thyme and parsley)	3-4
Poppy Seed or Sesame Seed	1 cup/250 mL all-purpose flour	1 cup/250 mL semolina	1/4 cup/50 mL whole poppy seeds or sesame seeds	3-4
Fennel	1 cup/250 mL all-purpose flour	1 cup/250 mL semolina	1/2 cup/125 mL yield puréed fennel (fresh fennel, tops and bottoms cut off, then blanched for 20 minutes and puréed very fine)	2
Leek	1 cup/250 mL all-purpose flour	1 cup/250 mL semolina	1/2 cup/125 mL yield puréed leeks (leeks washed and cleaned, discarding the root and leaves — use just the white part; then boiled for 15 minutes and puréed very fine)	2
Peach	1 cup/250 mL all-purpose flour	1 cup/250 mL semolina	1 cup/250 mL yield puréed peaches (fresh peaches, skin on, puréed very fine with 2 tbsp./25 mL milk)	2
Apricot	1 cup/250 mL all-purpose flour	1 cup/250 mL semolina	1 cup/250 mL yield puréed apricots (fresh apricots, skin on, puréed very fine with 2 tbsp./25 mL milk)	2
Lemon	1 cup/250 mL all-purpose flour	1 cup/250 mL semolina	juice of 1 medium fresh lemon	2

Garlic	1 cup/250 mL all-purpose flour	1 cup/250 mL semolina	3 medium cloves garlic, minced very fine	4
Saffron	1 cup/250 mL all-purpose flour	1 cup/250 mL semolina	5 tsp./25 mL saffron powder	4
Curry	1 cup/250 mL all-purpose flour	1 cup/250 mL semolina	5 tsp./25 mL curry powder	4

Pasta Verde

Green Olive	1 cup/250 mL all-purpose flour	1 cup/250 mL semolina	1/2 cup/125 mL yield puréed green olives (olives halved, pitted, chopped, then puréed very fine)	2
Broccoli	1 cup/250 mL all-purpose flour	1 cup/250 mL semolina	1/2 cup/125 mL yield puréed broccoli (broccoli boiled for 20 minutes, then puréed very fine with 2 tbsp./25 mL milk)	2
Spinach	1 cup/250 mL all-purpose flour	1 cup/250 mL semolina	1/2 cup/125 mL fresh spinach, washed and stemmed, chopped, then puréed very fine	2
Swiss Chard	1 cup/250 mL all-purpose flour	1 cup/250 mL semolina	1/2 cup/125 mL fresh Swiss chard, washed and stemmed, chopped, then puréed very fine	2
Seaweed	1 cup/250 mL all-purpose flour	1 cup/250 mL semolina	1/2 cup/125 mL seaweed, soaked in water for 30 minutes, then boiled in water with 1/4 cup/50 mL red wine vinegar, strained, chopped, then puréed very fine	2
Artichoke	1 cup/250 mL all-purpose flour	1 cup/250 mL semolina	1/2 cup/125 mL yield puréed artichoke hearts (trim spiky tips of leaves and remove any brown outer leaves, then boil artichokes	2

Allow artichokes to cool, then remove leaves until you reach the heart. Clean artichokes of spiny parts and hair, then purée hearts very fine with 1 tsp./5 mL olive oil—or use canned artichoke hearts, drained, chopped and puréed very fine, but if you use canned artichoke hearts, the colour will be lighter — a pale yellowish green)

Green Bell Pepper	1 cup/250 mL all-purpose flour	1 cup/250 mL semolina	1/2 cup/125 mL yield puréed green bell peppers (peppers washed, halved, seeded, julienned and sautéed in olive oil until soft, then drained and puréed very fine)	2
Avocado	1 cup/250 mL all-purpose flour	1 cup/250 mL semolina	1/2 cup/125 mL yield puréed avocado (avocado peeled, pitted, chopped and puréed very fine)	2
Celery	1 cup/250 mL all-purpose flour	1 cup/250 mL semolina	1/2 cup/125 mL yield puréed celery (celery peeled and chopped, then puréed very fine)	2
Cilantro	1 cup/250 mL all-purpose flour	1 cup/250 mL semolina	1/4 cup/50 mL fresh cilantro, chopped, then puréed very fine	3-4
Sorel	1 cup/250 mL all-purpose flour	1 cup/250 mL semolina	1/4 cup/50 mL fresh sorel — the leaves only, chopped, then puréed very fine	3-4
Dill	1 cup/250 mL all-purpose flour	1 cup/250 mL semolina	1/4 cup/50 mL fresh dill, very finely chopped	3-4
Sage	1 cup/250 mL all-purpose flour	1 cup/250 mL semolina	1/4 cup/50 mL fresh sage, very finely chopped	3-4
Watercress	1 cup/250 mL all-purpose flour	1 cup/250 mL semolina	1/4 cup/50 mL fresh watercress, very finely chopped	3-4
Parsley	1 cup/250 mL all-purpose flour	1 cup/250 mL semolina	1/4 cup/50 mL fresh parsley, very finely chopped	3-4
Mint	1 cup/250 mL all-purpose flour	1 cup/250 mL semolina	1/4 cup/50 mL fresh mint, very finely chopped	3-4
Chive	1 cup/250 mL all-purpose flour	1 cup/250 mL semolina	1/4 cup/50 mL fresh chives, very finely chopped	3-4
Basil	1 cup/250 mL all-purpose flour	1 cup/250 mL semolina	1/4 cup/50 mL fresh basil, very finely chopped	3-4

Pasta Rosa

Beet	1 cup/250 mL all-purpose flour	1 cup/250 mL semolina	1/2 cup/125 mL yield puréed beets (fresh beets, tops and bottoms cut off, washed and boiled for 45 minutes, then peeled, quartered and puréed very fine with 2 tbsp./25 mL milk)	2
Tomato	1 cup/250 mL all-purpose flour	1 cup/250 mL semolina	1/2 cup/125 mL tomato paste	2

Carrot	1 cup/250 mL all-purpose flour	1 cup/250 mL semolina	1/2 cup/125 mL yield puréed carrots (fresh carrots, tops cut off, washed and boiled for 15-20 minutes until very tender, then puréed very fine)	2
Radicchio	1 cup/250 mL all-purpose flour	1 cup/250 mL semolina	1/2 cup/125 mL yield puréed radicchio (core removed, washed, chopped, then puréed very fine with 1 tbsp./15 mL olive oil)	2
Red Bell Peppers	1 cup/250 mL all-purpose flour	1 cup/250 mL semolina	1/2 cup/125 mL yield puréed red bell peppers (peppers washed, halved, seeded, julienned and sautéed in olive oil until soft, then drained and puréed very fine)	2

Pasta Nera

Squid or Cuttlefish Ink	1 cup/250 mL all-purpose flour	1 cup/250 mL semolina	5 tbsp./75 mL squid or cuttlefish ink mixed with 3 tbsp./50 mL olive oil. If you cannot obtain squid ink, which comes in a vial, or cuttlefish ink, you can locate the ink in the vein of the intestine of the squid or cuttlefish, and in the eye of the squid. You will need 10-15 lbs./5-7 kg of squid or cuttlefish to give you enough ink. When you are cleaning the squid or cuttlefish, cut vein, and eye of the squid, with a sharp knife and drain ink into a bowl, then mix with 3 tbsp./50 mL olive oil	4
	all-purpose flour	semolina	1/2 cup/125 mL yield puréed black olives (olives halved, pitted, chopped, then puréed very fine)	2
Black Truffle	1 cup/250 mL all-purpose flour	1 cup/250 mL semolina	1 (75 g) tube of truffle paste — or 1 (.45 oz./12.5 g) can black truffles, and liquid, puréed very fine	3-4

How to Cook Pasta

How to Cook Pasta—illustrated above is a 7 qt./7 L pot, salt and a wooden spoon, your basic tools for cooking pasta.

How to Cook Pasta

For 1 lb./500 g

4 qts./4 L cold water
1 1/2 tbsp./20 mL salt

Put water in a 7 qt./7 L pot. Add salt to water. Bring water to a boil and add pasta. Cook pasta al dente — time varies according to type of pasta (see below). Drain and rinse under cold running water. Set aside.

When Cooking Pasta, Follow These Simple Rules:

1.) The most important thing about cooking pasta is to cook it in a pot *large enough* for the water to circulate once it's boiling. For 1 lb./500 g of pasta, we recommend at least a 7 qt./7 L pot.

2.) Never leave the kitchen while pasta is cooking in the pot. Watch over it carefully. Pasta takes so little time to cook, you shouldn't have to leave the kitchen.

3.) Add salt to the water approximately 2 minutes before you add the pasta. Two minutes will allow enough time for the salt to dissolve in the water.

4.) Make sure that the water is *rapidly* boiling before you add the pasta.

5.) Use a wooden spoon to stir the pasta in the pot. Always stir gently.

6.) Cook pasta *al dente,* which means "firm to the bite." Begin to test the pasta 2 minutes after it is in the pot, unless it is homemade pasta. Homemade pasta can take as little as 1 minute to cook. If homemade pasta is stored for a day or two, or you are using fresh store-bought pasta, which probably has dried for a day or two, in most cases, it will take 3-5 minutes to cook. Consult cooking times below. Do *not* overcook pasta. There should be no flour taste to your pasta when cooked; but, it should not be mushy or sticky.

7.) Rinse and toss pasta in a colander in any recipe where pasta is being added to the sauce. In most recipes in this book, pasta *is* being added to the sauce. Rinse pasta as soon as it has cooked *al dente.* Use cold running water and do *not* overrinse. Do *not* overdrain. Pasta should be wet, still dripping with water, when you add it to your sauce.

8.) Cook sauce in a skillet large enough to contain 1 lb./500 g cooked pasta *and* sauce. We recommend a rimmed skillet at least 14-16 inches/ 35-40 cm in diameter.

the other way around.

10.) Toss and heat — to warm the pasta — then serve.

Approximate Cooking Times for Pasta Used in This Book:

	Fresh Pasta	Packaged Pasta
Agnolotti	12-15 minutes	Always use fresh
Cannelloni	3-5 minutes (before stuffing)	Always use fresh
Capelli d'Angelo	1 minute	2 1/2 minutes
Farfalle	Use packaged	5-7 minutes
Fettuccine	3-5 minutes	5-7 minutes

	Fresh Pasta	**Packaged Pasta**
Fusilli	3-5 minutes	5-7 minutes
Gnocchi	3 minutes	5 minutes
Lasagna	3-5 minutes (before layering)	Use fresh (5-7 minutes, if packaged — before layering)
Linguine	3-5 minutes	5-7 minutes
Lumache	3-5 minutes	5-7 minutes for the medium size shells; 10-15 minutes for the large shells
Macaroni	3-5 minutes	5-7 minutes
Paglia e Fieno	For capelli d'angelo, 1 minute; for fettuccine, 3-5 minutes	For capelli d'angelo, 2 1/2 minutes; for fettuccine, 5-7 minutes
Pappardelle	3-5 minutes	5-7 minutes
Penne	3-5 minutes	7-9 minutes
Rigatoni	3-5 minutes	10-15 minutes
Risotto	Use packaged	15-18 minutes
Rotini	3-5 minutes	5-7 minutes
Sedanini	3-5 minutes	5-7 minutes
Spaghetti	3-5 minutes	5-7 minutes
Tortellini	7-10 minutes	10-15 minutes
Ziti	3-5 minutes	5-7 minutes

Basic Stocks & Sauces

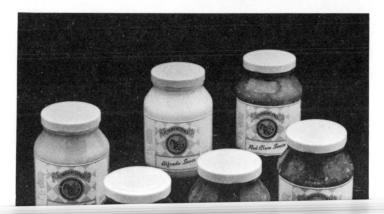

Basic Stocks and Sauces—illustrated above are the 6 varieties of sauces that are available through Umbertino's: White Clam Sauce, Alfredo Sauce, Red Clam Sauce, Tomato Sauce, Meat Sauce and Pesto Sauce. Try Umbertino's Tomato Sauce and Meat Sauce in place of the two recipes in this section.

Salsa Bianca
Béchamel Sauce

Makes 4 cups/1 L

1/2 cup/125 mL unsalted butter 1/2 cup/125 mL all-purpose flour	*Melt butter in a saucepan. Remove saucepan from heat and add flour, a little at a time, stirring constantly with a whisk to form a roux.*
4 cups/1 L milk	*Return saucepan to heat and add milk to roux, a little at a time at first, stirring constantly with a whisk to make a paste. Once you have made a paste, add remaining milk more quickly, continuing to stir until milk is well blended with the roux.*
salt white pepper 1/4 tsp./1 mL ground nutmeg	*Season with salt, pepper and nutmeg.*
	Simmer on low heat for 2-3 minutes, stirring constantly.

Béchamel Sauce is used in many recipes in this book. Make it fresh in any recipe that calls for it. The proportions are: equal parts unsalted butter and flour to milk. The ratio is approximately 4 to 1: 4 parts milk to 1 part unsalted butter and flour. Make Béchamel Sauce before you begin any recipe that calls for it and warm when needed.

Salsa di Carne
Meat Sauce

Makes 6 cups/1.5 L

1 large white onion, finely chopped 3 tbsp./50 mL olive oil	*Sauté onion in olive oil in a skillet for 1 minute until soft and transparent.*
1 lb./500 g lean ground beef 4 cloves garlic, finely chopped	*Add ground beef and garlic to skillet and sauté for approximately 5 minutes until beef is evenly browned.*
6 firm, ripe tomatoes, finely chopped 2 tbsp./25 mL tomato paste 1 cup/250 mL dry red wine 1 cup/250 mL beef consommé (see p. 20)	*Add tomatoes, tomato paste, red wine and beef consommé to skillet and stir until well blended. Simmer, uncovered, for 1 hour, stirring frequently.*

Meat Sauce is used in a few recipes in this book. Make it ahead in any recipe that calls for it — or have it on hand. Meat Sauce can be stored in your refrigerator in a sealed plastic container for approximately 1 week.

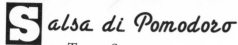alsa di Pomodoro

Tomato Sauce

Makes 4 cups/1 L

1 large white onion, finely chopped 1 tbsp./15 mL unsalted butter 1 tbsp./15 mL olive oil	Sauté onion in butter and olive oil in a saucepan for 1-2 minutes until soft and transparent.
1 stalk celery, finely chopped 1 medium carrot, finely chopped	Add celery and carrot to saucepan and sauté for approximately 5 minutes.
1 (28 oz./796 mL) can of peeled Italian tomatoes, finely chopped, and liquid 2 tbsp./25 mL tomato paste 2 cloves garlic, minced 1 bay leaf 1 tsp./5 mL fresh oregano, finely chopped 1/2 tsp./2 mL fresh basil, finely chopped 1 whole clove, crushed 1 tbsp./15 mL sugar 1/2 cup/125 mL dry red wine	Add tomatoes, tomato liquid, tomato paste, garlic, bay leaf, oregano, basil, cloves, sugar and red wine to saucepan and simmer, uncovered, on low heat for approximately 1 hour.
salt freshly ground black pepper	Season with salt and pepper to taste.
	Strain sauce through a fine sieve. This tomato sauce should be rich, thick sauce. If sauce is too thin after straining, return to saucepan and continue to simmer until sauce reaches the correct consistency. If sauce is too thick, add a little water.
1 tbsp./15 mL olive oil	When sauce has reached the correct consistency, remove saucepan from heat. Add olive oil to top, but do not mix in. Allow sauce to cool.

4 hours.

Tomato Sauce is used in many recipes in this book. Make it ahead and always have it on hand. Tomato Sauce can be stored in your refrigerator in a sealed plastic container for approximately 1 week.

Consommé di Manzo

Beef Consommé

1 beef knuckle bone, with a little meat on the bone — or equivalent weight of soup bones, with the meat on	*Chop knuckle bone or soup bones into large pieces and put in a pot.*
1 large white onion, finely chopped 1 small carrot, ground 1 stalk celery, ground 1 small leek, washed and cleaned, then ground	*Add vegetables to pot.*
3 qts./3 L cold water	*Add water to pot and bring to a boil. Skim froth from top.*
1 bay leaf 1/8 tsp./pinch of fresh sage 1/8 tsp./pinch of fresh thyme	*Season with bay leaf, sage and thyme.*
	Reduce heat and simmer on low heat for 2-3 hours.
	Strain through a sieve lined with a linen or muslin cloth.
salt white pepper	*Season with salt and pepper to taste.*

Beef Consommé is used in only a few recipes in this book. Make it ahead in any recipe that calls for it — or have it on hand. Beef Consommé can be stored in your refrigerator in sealed plastic container for approximately 1 week.

Consommé di Pollo

Chicken Consommé

1 chicken carcass	*Wash chicken bones under cold water. Chop carcass into large pieces and put in a pot.*
1 small white onion, chopped 1 small carrot, chopped 1 stalk celery, chopped	*Add vegetables to pot.*
3 qts./3 L cold water	*Add water to pot and bring to a boil. Skim froth from top.*
1 bay leaf 1/8 tsp./pinch of fresh thyme, finely chopped	*Season with bay leaf and thyme.*
	Reduce heat and simmer on low heat for 2-3 hours.

Strain through a sieve lined with a linen or muslin cloth.

salt
white pepper

Season with salt and pepper to taste.

Chicken Consommé is used in almost every second recipe in this book. Make it ahead and always have it on hand. Chicken Consommé can be stored in your refrigerator in a sealed plastic container for approximately 1 week.

Consommé di Pesce

Makes 4 cups/1 L

Fish Consommé

2 lbs./1 kg white fish bones, and trimmings
1 large white onion, diced
1/2 stalk celery, diced
3 stalks fresh parsley
1 bay leaf
3/4 cup/175 mL dry white wine

Put fish bones and trimmings, onion, celery, parsley, bay leaf and white wine in a pot.

2 qts./2 L cold water

Add water to pot and bring to a boil, then reduce heat and simmer on low heat for approximately 2 hours.

Strain stock through a sieve lined with a linen or muslin cloth.

salt
white pepper

Season with salt and pepper to taste.

Fish Consommé is used in several recipes in this book. Make it ahead in any recipe that calls for it — or have it on hand. Fish Consommé can be stored in your refrigerator in a sealed plastic container for approximately 1 week.

Agnolotti

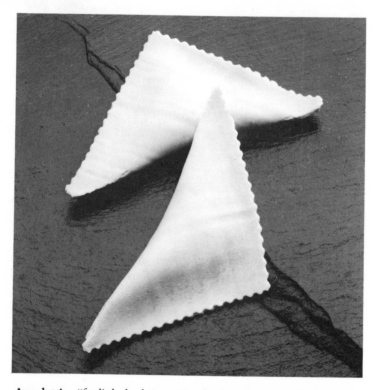

Agnolotti — "fat little lambs" — triangle shaped pasta made by stuffing 4 inch/10 cm uncooked fresh pasta squares, folding the squares in half and sealing them, then cooking them in boiling water for 12–15 minutes.

Agnolotti Bianco-Verde Salsa Rosa

Agnolotti Stuffed with Ricotta Cheese and Spinach in a Light Tomato Sauce

16-24 uncooked fresh egg or spinach pasta squares, cut in 4 inch/10 cm squares

Stuffing:

3 bunches of fresh spinach, washed and stemmed
1 tbsp./15 mL unsalted butter
1 tbsp./15 mL dry white wine

Heat butter and white wine in a saucepan. Add spinach and cover saucepan. Cook spinach for 3-4 minutes, stirring once. Drain saucepan. Allow spinach to cool, then finely chop. Put spinach in a bowl.

1 cup/250 mL Ricotta cheese
2 egg yolks
1/4 cup/50 mL Parmesan cheese, freshly grated

Add Ricotta cheese, egg yolks and Parmesan cheese to spinach in bowl and mix together thoroughly.

salt
freshly ground black pepper
1/8 tsp./pinch of ground nutmeg

Season with salt, pepper and nutmeg.

Lay uncooked pasta squares on a clean work surface and put approximately 1 tbsp./15 mL of stuffing mixture in the centre of each pasta square.

1 egg yolk, beaten

Brush two sides of each pasta square with egg yolk and fold from opposite corner to form triangle-shaped agnolotti. Leaving agnolotti on the work surface, press the two square edges together with a fork or seal with a serrated dough cutter so that no water can enter while agnolotti are cooking.

4 qts./4 L cold water

Put water in a 5 qt./5 L pot. Add salt to

pot one at a time, being careful that they do not unfold or break. Cook agnolotti al dente: 12-15 minutes for fresh agnolotti. Stir once while cooking to make sure that no agnolotti are sticking to the bottom of the pot. When agnolotti are cooked al dente, using a slotted spoon, pick them up one at a time. Do not rinse. Put agnolotti on a warm serving platter and keep warm.

Sauce:

3 cups/750 mL tomato sauce (see p. 19)

Purée tomato sauce in a blender or food processor, then put in a saucepan and heat.

(cont'd over)

2 tbsp./25 mL unsalted butter	*Add butter to tomato sauce and blend in. Cook for 3-4 minutes until sauce is smooth and velvety.*
salt freshly ground black pepper	*Adjust seasoning with salt and pepper to taste.*
1/4 cup/50 mL Parmesan cheese, freshly grated 1 tbsp./15 mL fresh parsley, finely chopped	*Spoon sauce over agnolotti on warm serving platter. Sprinkle with Parmesan cheese and chopped fresh parsley and serve.*

gnolotti con Ripieno di Capesante   Serves 4-6

Agnolotti Stuffed with Scallops

16-24 uncooked fresh pasta squares, cut in 4 inch/10 cm squares

Stuffing:

1 tbsp./15 mL shallot, finely chopped 2 tbsp./25 mL unsalted butter	*Sauté shallot in butter in a skillet for 1 minute until soft and transparent.*
1/2 lb./250 g fresh scallops, washed and diced	*Add scallops to skillet and sauté for approximately 3 minutes.*
salt white pepper juice of 1/2 lemon 1 tbsp./15 mL fresh parsley, finely chopped	*Season with salt, pepper, lemon juice and parsley.*
2 tbsp./25 mL dry white wine	*Add white wine to skillet and reduce by simmering for approximately 1 minute.*
	Remove skillet from heat. Put scallop mixture in a bowl and allow mixture to cool.
2 tbsp./25 mL Parmesan cheese, freshly grated 1 tbsp./15 mL fine breadcrumbs 2 egg yolks 2 tbsp./25 mL whipping cream	*Add Parmesan cheese, breadcrumbs, egg yolks and cream to scallop mixture in bowl and mix together thoroughly.*
salt white pepper	*Season with salt and pepper to taste.*
	Lay uncooked pasta squares on a clean work surface and put approximately 1 tbsp./15 mL of stuffing mixture in the centre of each pasta square.
1 egg yolk, beaten	*Brush two sides of each pasta square with egg yolk and fold from opposite corner to form triangle-shaped agnolotti. Leaving agnolotti on the*

work surface, press the two square edges together with a fork or seal with a serrated dough cutter so that no water can enter while agnolotti are cooking.

4 qts./4 L cold water 1 1/2 tbsp./20 mL salt	Put water in a 5 qt./5 L pot. Add salt to water. Bring water to a boil and add agnolotti to pot one at a time, being careful that they do not unfold or break. Cook agnolotti al dente: 12-15 minutes for fresh agnolotti. Stir once while cooking to make sure that no agnolotti are sticking to the bottom of the pot. When agnolotti are cooked al dente, using a slotted spoon, pick them up one at a time. Do not rinse. Put agnolotti on a warm serving platter and keep warm.

Sauce:

1 tbsp./15 mL unsalted butter 1 cup/250 mL whipping cream 1/4 cup/50 mL Parmesan cheese, freshly grated	Melt butter in a skillet, then add cream and Parmesan cheese and mix together. Cook until sauce thickens slightly.
salt white pepper	Season with salt and pepper to taste.
1 tbsp./15 mL fresh parsley, finely chopped	Spoon sauce over agnolotti on warm serving platter. Sprinkle with chopped fresh parsley and serve.

 Agnolotti Cinesi Serves 4-6

Agnolotti Stuffed with Oysters, Shallots and Ginger

16-24 uncooked fresh pasta squares, cut in 4 inch/10 cm squares

1 tbsp./15 mL shallot, finely chopped 2 tbsp./25 mL unsalted butter	Sauté shallot in butter in a skillet for 1 minute until soft and transparent.
1/4 tsp./1 mL fresh ginger, minced zest of 1/2 lemon	Add ginger and lemon zest to skillet and gently stir.
1/4 cup/50 mL dry white wine	Add white wine to skillet and reduce by simmering for 1-2 minutes.
16-24 fresh oysters, shucked and chopped	Add oysters to skillet and sauté for approximately 2 mintues.

(cont'd over)

2 tbsp./25 mL whipping cream 1 tbsp./15 mL unsalted butter	*Add cream and butter to skillet and stir until well blended. Simmer for approximately 2 minutes until mixture thickens.*
salt freshly ground black pepper	*Season with salt and pepper to taste. (Be careful with the salt as oysters may be salty to begin with.) Set stuffing mixture aside and allow it to cool.*
	Lay uncooked pasta squares on a clean work surface and put approximately 1 tbsp./15 mL of stuffing mixture in the centre of each pasta square.
1 egg yolk, beaten	*Brush two sides of each pasta square with egg yolk and fold from opposite corner to form triangle-shaped agnolotti. Leaving agnolotti on the work surface, press the two square edges together with a fork or seal with a serrated dough cutter so that no water can enter while agnolotti are cooking.*
4 qts./4 L cold water 1 1/2 tbsp./20 mL salt	*Put water in a 5 qt./5 L pot. Add salt to water. Bring water to a boil and add agnolotti to pot one at a time, being careful that they do not unfold or break. Cook agnolotti al dente: 12-15 minutes for fresh agnolotti. Stir once while cooking to make sure that no agnolotti are sticking to the bottom of the pot. When agnolotti are cooked al dente, using a slotted spoon, pick them up one at a time. Do not rinse. Put agnolotti on a warm serving platter and keep warm.*

Sauce:

1 cup/250 mL fresh mushrooms, cleaned and thinly sliced 1 tbsp./15 mL unsalted butter	*Sauté mushrooms in butter in a skillet for approximately 3 minutes.*
1/4 cup/50 mL dry white wine juice of 1/2 lemon	*Add white wine and lemon juice to skillet and reduce by simmering for 1-2 minutes.*
1 cup/250 mL whipping cream	*Add cream to skillet and stir until well blended. Simmer for 2-3 minutes until sauce thickens slightly.*
salt freshly ground black pepper	*Season with salt and pepper to taste.*
4 leaves of fresh spinach, washed and stemmed, then julienned	*Spoon sauce over agnolotti on warm serving platter. Sprinkle with julienned fresh spinach and serve.*

Cannelloni

Cannelloni—"large reeds"—pasta made by stuffing 4 inch/10 cm cooked fresh pasta squares, then baking in a pan in the oven for 30 minutes.

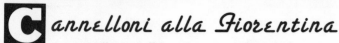

Cannelloni alla Fiorentina

Makes 30 Cannelloni

Cannelloni Stuffed with Meat and Spinach

Cook 30 fresh egg noodle pasta squares, cut in 4 inch/10 cm squares, al dente: approximately 3 mintues for fresh egg noodle pasta squares (to cook pasta, see p. 15). Drop pasta squares one at a time into boiling water to prevent sticking.

Stuffing:

3 lbs./1.5 kg ground veal 1 tbsp./15 mL unsalted butter	*Sauté ground veal in butter in a skillet for 5 minutes until veal turns white, then put in a bowl.*
2 bunches of fresh spinach, washed and stemmed	*Blanch spinach in a pot of boiling water for 2 minutes, then drain and squeeze dry. Finely chop spinach. Add spinach to veal in bowl and mix together. Set aside.*
1 large white onion, ground 1 tsp./5 mL unsalted butter 1 tsp./5 mL olive oil	*Sauté onion in butter and olive oil in a skillet for 1-2 minutes until soft and transparent.*
1 large carrot, ground 2 stalks celery, ground 3 cloves garlic, finely chopped	*Add carrot, celery and garlic to skillet and sauté for 5 minutes, then add vegetables to spinach and veal in bowl and mix together.*
4 eggs 1 cup/250 mL Béchamel sauce (see p. 18) 1 cup/250 mL Parmesan cheese, freshly grated 1/4 cup/50 mL fine breadcrumbs	*Add eggs, Béchamel sauce, Parmesan cheese and breadcrumbs to vegetable, spinach and veal mixture in bowl and mix together thoroughly.*
salt freshly ground black pepper 1/8 tsp./pinch of ground nutmeg	*Season with salt, pepper and nutmeg.*
	Pre-heat oven to 350°F/180°C.
	Put a portion of the stuffing mixture on each pasta square and roll up to make cannelloni.
1 cup/250 mL whipping cream	*Cover the bottom of a casserole dish with cream and put cannelloni in dish, side by side.*
2 cups/500 mL Béchamel sauce (see p. 18) 1 cup/250 mL Parmesan cheese, freshly grated	*Cover cannelloni with Béchamel sauce and sprinkle with Parmesan cheese. Put casserole dish in oven at 350°F/180°C and bake for 30 minutes until Béchamel sauce is bubbling.*
	Serve on warm plates.

If you're not using the cannelloni the same day, you may freeze what you do not use.

Cannelloni alla Sorrentina

Cannelloni Stuffed with Tomatoes, Eggplant and Zucchini in a Light Tomato Sauce

Cook 18 fresh egg noodle pasta squares, cut in 4 inch/10 cm squares, al dente: approximately 3 minutes for fresh egg noodle pasta squares (to cook pasta, see p. 15). Drop pasta squares one at a time into boiling water to prevent sticking.

Stuffing:

1 medium white onion, chopped 2 tbsp./25 mL unsalted butter	*Sauté onion in butter in a skillet for 1 minute until soft and transparent.*
4 firm, ripe tomatoes, washed, chopped and seeded 1 medium eggplant, washed, dried and cubed 3 medium zucchini, washed, dried and cubed	*Add tomatoes, eggplant and zucchini to skillet and sauté for 10 minutes.*
4 tbsp./60 mL fresh basil, finely chopped 2 tbsp./25 mL fresh oregano, finely chopped 5 medium cloves garlic, finely chopped 1/4 cup/50 mL dry white wine	*Add basil, oregano, garlic and white wine to skillet and simmer for approximately 2 minutes. Vegetables should be cooked, but not mushy. Put vegetables in a bowl.*
4 egg yolks 1 cup/250 mL Mozzarella cheese, freshly grated 1 cup/250 mL fine breadcrumbs	*Add egg yolks, Mozzarella cheese and breadcrumbs to vegetables in bowl and mix together thoroughly.*
salt freshly ground black pepper	*Season with salt and pepper.*
	Pre-heat oven to 350°F/180°C.
	Put a portion of the stuffing mixture on each pasta square and roll up to make cannelloni.
1 cup/250 mL whipping cream	*Cover the bottom of a casserole dish with cream and put cannelloni in dish, side by side.*
4 cups/1 L tomato sauce (see p. 19) 1 cup/250 mL Parmesan cheese, freshly grated	*Cover cannelloni with tomato sauce and sprinkle with Parmesan cheese. Put casserole dish in oven at 350°F/180°C and bake for approximately 30 minutes.*
	Serve on warm plates.

If you're not using the cannelloni the same day, you may freeze what you do not use.

Cannelloni di Mare

Cannelloni Stuffed with Crab and Spinach

Cook 18 fresh egg noodle pasta squares, cut in 4 inch/10 cm squares, al dente: approximately 3 minutes for fresh egg noodle pasta squares (to cook pasta, see p. 15). Drop pasta squares one at a time into boiling water to prevent sticking.

Stuffing:

1 lb./500 g fresh crabmeat	*Put crabmeat in a bowl.*
2 bunches of fresh spinach, washed and stemmed	*Blanch spinach in a pot of boiling water for 2 minutes, then drain and squeeze dry. Finely chop spinach. Add spinach to crabmeat in bowl and mix together. Set aside.*
1 small white onion, ground 2 cloves garlic, finely chopped 1 tsp./5 mL unsalted butter 1 tsp./5 mL olive oil	*Sauté onion and garlic in butter and olive oil in a skillet for 1 minute until onion is soft and transparent. Add onion and garlic to spinach and crabmeat in bowl and mix together.*
2 eggs 1 cup/250 mL Béchamel sauce (see p. 18) 2 tbsp./25 mL fine breadcrumbs	*Add eggs, Béchamel sauce and breadcrumbs to spinach and crabmeat mixture in bowl and mix together thoroughly.*
salt freshly ground black pepper 1 tsp./5 mL fresh nutmeg, grated	*Season with salt, pepper and nutmeg.*
	Pre-heat oven to 350°F/180°C.
	Put a portion of the stuffing mixture on each pasta square and roll up to make cannelloni.
1 cup/250 mL whipping cream	*Cover the bottom of a casserole dish with cream and put cannelloni in dish, side by side.*
1 cup/250 mL Béchamel sauce (see p. 18) 1 cup/250 mL Parmesan cheese, freshly grated	*Cover cannelloni with Béchamel sauce and sprinkle with Parmesan cheese. Put casserole dish in oven at 350°F/180°C and bake for 30 minutes until Béchamel sauce is bubbling.*
	Serve on warm plates.

If you're not using the cannelloni the same day, you may freeze what you do not use, but do not keep too long in the freezer.

Capelli d'Angelo

Capelli d'Angelo—"angel hair"—long, thin, fine, round pasta—the same shape as spaghetti, only finer.

Capelli d' Angelo Basilico e Pomodoro *Serves 4-6*

Angel Hair with a Fillet of Tomatoes, Garlic, Basil and Parmesan Cheese

Cook 1 lb./500 g capelli d'angelo al dente: approximately 1 minute for fresh capelli d'angelo; approximately 2 1/2 minutes for packaged capelli d'angelo (to cook pasta, see p. 15).

Sauce:

2-3 firm, ripe tomatoes, eyes removed and scored "x" on top	*Blanch tomatoes in a pot of boiling water for 20 seconds, then plunge in cold water to stop the cooking. Peel, seed and julienne tomatoes. Set aside.*
2 medium cloves garlic, finely chopped 1 tbsp./15 mL unsalted butter	*Sauté garlic in butter in a skillet for 1 minute. (Be careful that you don't burn the garlic.)*
1/4 cup/50 mL dry white wine	*Add white wine to skillet and reduce by simmering for 1-2 minutes.*
1/3 cup/75 mL chicken consommé (see p. 21)	*Add chicken consommé to skillet and simmer for 2-3 minutes.*
1 1/2 tbsp./20 mL fresh basil, finely chopped 2 tbsp./25 mL unsalted butter	*Add tomatoes, basil and butter to skillet and stir until well blended. Cook for 2-3 minutes.*
salt freshly ground black pepper	*Season with salt and pepper to taste.*
	Add capelli d'angelo to sauce in skillet. Toss and heat.
1 cup/250 mL Parmesan cheese, freshly grated	*Gradually add Parmesan cheese to capelli d'angelo. Toss and heat.*
	Put capelli d'angelo on a warm serving platter or warm plates and serve.

Illustration #1 (page 33): Capelli d'Angelo Basilico e Pomodoro/Angel Hair with a Fillet of Tomatoes, Garlic, Basil and Mozzarella Cheese photographed against Rosa del Monte marble, courtesy of Quadra Stone Company Ltd.; plates courtesy of Umberto's Restaurants Ltd.

Capelli d'Angelo Mamma Delia

Angel Hair with a Julienne of Celery, Carrot and Leek, Fontina Cheese and Snow Peas

Cook 1 lb./500 g capelli d'angelo al dente: approximately 1 minute for fresh capelli d'angelo; approximately 2 1/2 minutes for packaged capelli d'angelo (to cook pasta, see p. 15).

Sauce:

1/2 cup/125 mL celery, julienned 1/2 cup/125 mL carrots, julienned 1/2 cup/125 mL leeks, washed and cleaned, then julienned — use just the white part 1 cup/250 mL fresh snow peas, julienned 1/2 cup/125 mL dry white wine 2 tbsp./25 mL unsalted butter	*Sauté vegetables in white wine and butter in a skillet for 2-3 minutes until they are tender, but firm.*
1/2 cup/125 mL whipping cream 1/2 cup/125 mL chicken consommé (see p. 21)	*Add cream and chicken consommé to skillet and gently stir until well blended. Simmer for 2-3 minutes until mixture thickens slightly.*
2 tbsp./25 mL unsalted butter	*Add butter to sauce in skillet and blend in. Simmer for 2 minutes more.*
salt freshly ground black pepper	*Season with salt and pepper to taste.*
	Add capelli d'angelo to sauce in skillet. Toss and heat.
1/2 cup/125 mL Fontina cheese, freshly grated	*Gradually add Fontina cheese to capelli d'angelo. Toss and heat.*
	Put capelli d'angelo on a warm serving platter or warm plates and serve.

Illustration #2 (page 34): Farfalle alla Diana/Farfalle with Three Mushrooms photographed against Breccia Tavire (Cocoa Dorado) marble, courtesy of Quadra Stone Company Ltd.; plate courtesy of Umberto's Restaurants Ltd.

Farfalle

Farfalle—"butterflies" or "bow ties"—rectangular pasta that has been cut with a serrated dough cutter and pinched. Always use packaged farfalle—it's easier than making your own.

Farfalle alla Diana

Farfalle with Three Mushrooms

Use packaged farfalle. Cook 1 lb./500 g farfalle al dente: 5-7 minutes for packaged farfalle (to cook pasta, see p. 15).

Sauce:

1/2 lb./250 g fresh Chanterelle mushrooms, cleaned and chopped — or 1 (14 oz./398 mL) can Chanterelle mushrooms, drained, reserving the liquid, then chopped (reserving 4-6 whole mushrooms for garnish) 1/2 lb./250 g fresh Porcini or Boletus mushrooms, cleaned and chopped — or 1/4 lb./125 g dried Morel mushrooms, soaked (see p. 97), reserving and straining the liquid (reserving 4-6 whole mushrooms for garnish) 1/8 lb./50 g fresh champignon mushrooms, cleaned and chopped (reserving 4-6 whole mushrooms for garnish) 1 tsp./5 mL shallot, finely chopped 3 tbsp./50 mL unsalted butter	*Sauté mushrooms and shallot in butter in a skillet for approximately 2 minutes.*
1/4 cup/50 mL dry white wine 2 tbsp./25 mL dry sherry	*Add white wine and sherry to skillet and reduce by simmering for 1-2 minutes.*
1 cup/250 mL whipping cream mushroom liquid (reserved above) (optional)	*Add cream to skillet and stir until well blended. Simmer for approximately 2 minutes until sauce thickens slightly. (If sauce is too thick, add mushroom liquid and blend in.)*
salt freshly ground black pepper	*Season with salt and pepper to taste.*
	Add farfalle to sauce in skillet. Toss and heat.
1/4 cup/50 mL Parmesan cheese, freshly grated	*Add Parmesan cheese to farfalle. Toss and heat.*
4-6 whole mushrooms of each kind (reserved above)	*Put farfalle on a warm serving platter or warm plates. Garnish with whole mushrooms (one of each kind) and serve.*

Farfalle alla Puttanesca

Serves 4-6

Farfalle with Tuna, Black Olives and Tomatoes

Use packaged farfalle. Cook 1 lb./500 g farfalle al dente: 5-7 minutes for packaged farfalle (to cook pasta, see p. 15).

Sauce:

1 shallot, finely chopped 1 whole clove garlic 2 tbsp./25 mL olive oil	*Sauté shallot and garlic in olive oil in a skillet for 1 minute until shallot is soft and transparent. Remove garlic from skillet.*
1 (28 oz./796 mL) can Italian tomatoes, and liquid 4 large whole leaves of fresh basil	*Put tomatoes, tomato liquid and basil together in a blender or food processor and purée.*
	Add puréed tomato mixture to skillet and cook for approximately 15 minutes.
1 (6.5 oz./184 g) can flaked white tuna, drained	*Crumble tuna into skillet and gently stir.*
10 Calamata black olives, halved and pitted	*Add olives to skillet and gently stir. Cook sauce for 5 minutes more.*
salt white pepper	*Season with salt and pepper to taste.*
	Add farfalle to sauce in skillet. Toss and heat.
4-6 leaves of fresh basil, julienned	*Put farfalle on a warm serving platter or warm plates. Sprinkle with julienned fresh basil and serve. Cheese not recommended.*

Farfalle alla Veneziana

Serves 4-6

Farfalle with Veal Liver and Onions

Use packaged farfalle. Cook 1 lb./500 g farfalle al dente: 5-7 minutes for packaged farfalle (to cook pasta, see p. 15).

Sauce:

1/2 of 1 medium white onion, julienned 3 tbsp./50 mL vegetable oil	*Sauté onion in vegetable oil in a skillet for 1 minute until soft and transparent.*
1/2 lb./250 g veal liver, julienned	*Season veal liver with salt and pepper. Lightly dust with flour. Add veal liver to onion in skillet and quickly sauté until liver is lightly browned.*
2 medium cloves garlic, finely chopped	*Add garlic to skillet and toss for 1 minute.*
1/4 cup/50 mL dry white wine	*Add white wine to skillet and reduce by simmering for 1-2 minutes.*

2/3 cup/150 mL whipping cream	Add cream to skillet and stir until well blended. Simmer for approximately 2 minutes until sauce thickens slightly.
salt freshly ground black pepper	Season with salt and pepper to taste.
	Add farfalle to sauce in skillet. Toss and heat.
4-6 tbsp./60-90 mL Parmesan cheese, freshly grated	Put farfalle on a warm serving platter or warm plates. Sprinkle with Parmesan cheese and serve.

 ## arfalle Salmonate

Serves 4-6

Farfalle with Salmon and Celery

Use packaged farfalle. Cook 1 lb./500 g farfalle al dente: 5-7 minutes for packaged farfalle (to cook pasta, see p. 15).

Sauce:

1/2 cup/125 mL celery, thinly sliced diagonally 2 tbsp./25 mL unsalted butter 2 tbsp./25 mL vegetable oil	Sauté celery in butter and vegetable oil in a skillet for 1 minute.
1/2 lb./250 g fillet of fresh salmon, julienned	Add salmon to skillet and sauté for approximately 1 minute.
1/4 cup/50 mL dry white wine	Add white wine to skillet and reduce by simmering for 1-2 minutes.
1/4 cup/50 mL whipping cream	Add cream to skillet and stir until well blended. Simmer for approximately 2 minutes until sauce thickens slightly. (If sauce is too thick, add more cream.)
salt white pepper	Season with salt and pepper to taste.
	Add farfalle to sauce in skillet. Toss and heat.
2 tbsp./25 mL fresh chives or green onion, finely chopped	Put farfalle on a warm serving platter or warm plates. Sprinkle with fresh chopped chives or green onion and serve. Cheese not recommended.

Fettuccine

Fettuccine—"little ribbons"—pasta that has been cut by hand or by machine 1/4 to 3/8 inches/.5 to 1 cm thick. Often made fresh, but available dried—straight or in coils or "nests." Fettuccine is virtually interchangeable with *tagliolini*, from the verb "tagliare," which means "to cut." Illustrated above is dried egg noodle fettuccine—in "nests."

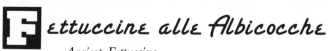ettuccine alle Albicocche

Apricot Fettuccine

Add puréed apricots to the flour and eggs when you're making the pasta (to make fresh coloured pasta, see p. 10). Cook fettuccine al dente: approximately 1 minute for fresh apricot fettuccine that you've just made (to cook pasta, see p. 15).

Sauce:

4 fresh apricots, skin on, halved and pitted 1 cup/250 mL dry white wine	*Poach apricots in white wine in a saucepan for 5 minutes.*
2 cups/500 mL whipping cream 1/2 cup/125 mL unsalted butter	*Add cream and butter to saucepan and simmer for 2-3 minutes until sauce thickens slightly.*
	Put sauce in a blender or food processor and purée. Using the bottom of a ladle or a rubber spatula, put sauce through a fine sieve into a skillet.
	Add apricot fettuccine to sauce in skillet. Toss and heat.
2 tbsp./25 mL crème fraîche (see below)	*Add crème fraîche to fettuccine and toss.*
1/8 tsp./pinch of lemon zest 1 fresh apricot, peeled, halved, pitted and julienned	*Put fettuccine on a warm serving platter or warm plates. Sprinkle with lemon zest. Garnish with julienned fresh apricot and serve.*

This pasta only works with fresh apricots. Or, make peach fettuccine. Add puréed peaches to the flour and eggs when you're making the pasta (to make fresh pasta, see p. 10) and use 1 fresh peach, peeled, halved and pitted, in sauce. If you don't want to make apricot or peach fettuccine, but want to use the sauce, cook egg fettuccine (3-5 minutes for fresh fettuccine; 5-7 minutes for packaged fettuccine) and add to sauce in skillet.

Crème Fraîche:

2 cups/500 mL whipping cream 1/2 cup/125 mL sour cream	*Using a whisk or a rubber spatula, mix cream and sour cream together in a plastic container. Let mixture sit out at room temperature overnight before using. Use amount needed, cover and store the rest in your refrigerator. Crème fraîche can be stored in your refrigerator in a sealed plastic container for approximately 1 week.*

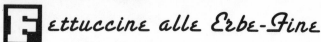

Fettuccine alle Erbe-Fine

Herbed Bell Pepper Fettuccine with Grilled Red Bell Pepper Sauce

Add finely chopped fresh herbs and 3 red bell peppers, washed, halved, seeded, chopped, sautéed and puréed to the flour and eggs when you're making the pasta (to make fresh coloured pasta, see p. 10). Cook 1 lb./500 g fettuccine al dente: approximately 1 minute for fresh herbed bell pepper fettuccine that you've just made (to cook pasta, see p. 15).

Sauce:

3 whole red bell peppers	*Grill peppers, turning them frequently, until they start to turn black. Rinse peppers under cold water, then peel, halve and seed. Put peppers in a saucepan.*
2 cups/500 mL dry white wine 1 shallot, finely chopped	*Add white wine and shallot to saucepan and simmer for approximately 3 minutes.*
	Put contents of saucepan in a blender or food processor and purée. Pour puréed pepper mixture into a skillet.
1/2 cup/125 mL whipping cream 1/2 cup/125 mL unsalted butter	*Add cream and butter to skillet and stir until well blended. Simmer for 2-3 minutes until sauce thickens slightly.*
salt white pepper	*Season with salt and pepper to taste.*
	Add herbed bell pepper fettuccine to sauce in skillet. Toss and heat.
2 tbsp./25 mL Parmesan cheese, freshly grated 1 tbsp./15 mL fresh parsley, finely chopped	*Put fettuccine on a warm serving platter or warm plates. Sprinkle with Parmesan cheese and chopped fresh parsley and serve.*

If you don't want to make herbed bell pepper fettuccine, but want to use the sauce, cook egg fettuccine (3-5 minutes for fresh fettuccine; 5-7 minutes for packaged fettuccine) and add to sauce in skillet.

Fettuccine con Prosciutto e Piselli

Fettuccine with Prosciutto and Peas

Cook 1 lb./500 g fettuccine al dente: 3-5 minutes for fresh fettuccine; 5-7 minutes for packaged fettuccine (to cook pasta, see p. 15).

Sauce:

1/3 cup/75 mL petits pois 2 tbsp./25 mL unsalted butter 2 tbsp./25 mL dry white wine	*Sauté peas in butter and white wine in a skillet for 2-3 minutes.*
2 cups/500 mL whipping cream	*Add cream to skillet and slowly bring to a boil.*

1/8 lb./50 g prosciutto, julienned	*Add prosciutto to skillet and cook for 2-3 minutes.*
salt freshly ground black pepper	*Season with salt and pepper to taste. (Use less salt than you normally would use. The prosciutto will give you some salt.)*
	Add fettuccine to sauce in skillet. Toss and heat.
1 cup/250 mL Parmesan cheese, freshly grated	*Gradually add Parmesan cheese to fettuccine. Toss and heat until cheese has melted.*
1/2 cup/125 mL Parmesan cheese, freshly grated 1 tbsp./15 mL fresh parsley, finely chopped	*Put fettuccine on a warm serving platter or warm plates. Sprinkle with Parmesan cheese and chopped fresh parsley and serve.*

F *ettuccine di Broccoli*   *Serves 4-6*

Broccoli Fettuccine

Add puréed broccoli to the flour and eggs when you're making the pasta (to make fresh coloured pasta, see p. 10). Cook 1 lb./500 g fettuccine al dente: approximately 1 minute for fresh broccoli fettuccine that you've just made (to cook fresh pasta, see p. 15).

Sauce:

1/2 lb./250 g broccoli — top half only 2 shallots, finely chopped 1 cup/250 mL dry white wine	*Simmer broccoli and shallots in white wine in a saucepan for 20 minutes.*
	Put contents of saucepan in a blender or food processor and purée. Pour puréed broccoli mixture into a skillet.
1 cup/250 mL whipping cream	*Add cream to skillet and stir until well blended. Simmer for 3-4 minutes until sauce thickens slightly.*
salt white pepper	*Season with salt and pepper to taste.*
	Add broccoli fettuccine to sauce in skillet. Toss and heat.
2-3 tbsp./25-50 mL Parmesan cheese, freshly grated 1 tbsp./15 mL fresh parsley, finely chopped	*Put fettuccine on a warm serving platter or warm plates. Sprinkle with Parmesan cheese and chopped fresh parsley and serve.*

If you don't want to make broccoli fettuccine, but want to use the sauce, cook egg fettuccine (3-5 minutes for fresh fettuccine; 5-7 minutes for packaged fettuccine) and add to sauce in skillet.

Fettuccine di Pomodoro

Tomato Fettuccine

Serves 4-6

Add tomato paste to the flour and eggs when you're making the pasta (to make fresh coloured pasta, see p. 10). Cook 1 lb./500 g fettuccine al dente: approximately 1 minute for fresh tomato fettuccine that you've just made (to cook pasta, see p. 15).

Sauce:

2 shallots, finely chopped 1 whole clove garlic 3 tbsp./50 mL olive oil	*Sauté shallots and garlic in olive oil in a skillet for 1-2 minutes until shallots are light brown.*
1/2 lb./250 g fresh wild Japanese shiitake mushrooms, cleaned and chopped — or 1/2 lb./250 g fresh champignon mushrooms, cleaned and chopped	*Add mushrooms to skillet and sauté for approximately 2 minutes.*
a splash of dry white wine 3 tbsp./50 mL fresh chives, finely chopped	*Add white wine and chives to skillet and simmer for approximately 1 minute.*
3 firm, ripe tomatoes, concassé	*Add tomatoes to skillet and cook for 1-2 minutes.*
salt white pepper	*Season with salt and pepper to taste.*
	Add tomato fettuccine to sauce in skillet. Toss and heat.
2 tbsp./25 mL Parmesan cheese, freshly grated	*Put fettuccine on a warm serving platter or warm plates. Sprinkle with Parmesan cheese and serve.*

If you don't want to make tomato fettuccine, but want to use the sauce, cook egg fettuccine (3-5 minutes for fresh fettuccine; 5-7 minutes for packaged fettuccine) and add to sauce in skillet.

Fettuccine di Salvia

Sage Fettuccine

Serves 4-6

Add finely chopped fresh sage to the flour and eggs when you're making the pasta (to make fresh coloured pasta, see p. 10). Cook 1 lb./500 g fettuccine al dente: approximately 1 minute for fresh sage fettuccine that you've just made (to cook pasta, see p. 15).

Sauce:

2/3 cup/150 mL unsalted butter 7 leaves of fresh sage, finely chopped — or 3 tsp./15 mL dry sage 1 shallot, finely chopped 2 tbsp./25 mL dry white wine	*Make a sage butter by mixing butter, sage, shallot and white wine together in a bowl with your hands until butter is soft.*

1/4 cup/50 mL dry white wine	Heat white wine in a skillet, then add sage butter. Allow butter to melt and, using a whisk, stir until well blended.
1/4 cup/50 mL chicken consommé (see p. 21)	Add chicken consommé to skillet and, continuing to use a whisk, stir until well blended. Simmer for approximately 2 minutes until sauce thickens slightly.
white pepper	Season with pepper only.
	Add sage fettuccine to sauce in skillet. Toss and heat.
4-6 tbsp./60-90 mL Parmesan cheese, freshly grated	Put fettuccine on a warm serving platter or warm plates. Sprinkle with Parmesan cheese and serve.

If you don't want to make sage fettuccine, but want to use the sauce, cook egg fettuccine (3-5 minutes for fresh fettuccine; 5-7 minutes for packaged fettuccine) and add to sauce in skillet.

ettuccine Nere

Serves 4-6

Black Fettuccine with Shrimp Sauce

Add squid ink or the ink of the cuttlefish to the flour and eggs when you're making the pasta (to make fresh coloured pasta, see p. 10). Use shrimp shells (the shells only) to make a pink shrimp sauce. Reserve shells when you cook shrimp some other time — or buy fresh shrimp, peel and clean them; reserve shells and freeze the shrimp. Cook 1 lb./500 g fettuccine al dente: approximately 1 minute for fresh black fettuccine that you've just made (to cook pasta, see p. 15).

Sauce:

1 shallot, finely chopped 2 tbsp./25 mL olive oil	Sauté shallot in olive oil in a skillet for 1 minute until soft and transparent.
1 white onion, chopped 4 stalks celery, chopped 3 medium carrots, chopped 1/2 lb./250 g shrimp shells — the shells only 1/2 cup/125 mL dry white wine	Add vegetables, shrimp shells and white wine to skillet and sauté for 10 minutes.
1 (28 oz./796 mL) can Italian tomatoes, and liquid	Add tomatoes and tomato liquid to skillet and cook for 15 minutes.
	Put contents of skillet in a food processor or food grinder and grind, then using the bottom of a ladle or a rubber spatula, put mixture through a fine sieve into a skillet.
1/4 cup/50 mL whipping cream	Add cream to skillet and stir until well blended. Simmer for approximately 2 minutes.
fish consommé (see p. 20)	Add fish stock to skillet until sauce reaches desired consistency. Simmer for approximately 2 minutes.

(cont'd over)

Add black fettuccine to sauce in skillet. Toss and heat.

16 large fresh scallops,
washed and halved
— or bay scallops
16-24 pink or green peppercorns
a splash of dry white wine

Put fettuccine on a warm serving platter or warm plates. Poach scallops and pink or green peppercorns in white wine in a skillet for 30 seconds. Garnish with poached scallops and pink or green peppercorns and serve.

Fettuccine Primavera

Serves 4-6

Fettuccine with Fresh Vegetables

Cook 1 lb./500 g fettuccine al dente: 3-5 minutes for fresh fettuccine; 5-7 minutes for packaged fettuccine (to cook pasta, see p. 15).

Sauce:

2 firm, ripe tomatoes, eyes removed and scored "x" on top

Blanch tomatoes in a pot of boiling water for 20 seconds, then plunge in cold water to stop the cooking. Peel, seed and julienne tomatoes. Set aside.

Pre-heat oven to 400°F/200°C.

1 red bell pepper

Put pepper in a casserole dish. Put casserole dish in oven at 400°F/200°C and bake for 15-20 minutes. Remove casserole dish from oven. Allow pepper to cool, then peel, seed and julienne. Set aside.

1 small carrot, julienned
1 small zucchini, julienned
1/2 cup/125 mL broccoli florets
1/2 cup/125 mL cauliflower florets
1/2 cup/125 mL fresh snow peas
2 cloves garlic, finely chopped
3 tbsp./50 mL unsalted butter

Sauté tomatoes, pepper, carrot, zucchini, broccoli and cauliflower florets, snow peas and garlic in butter in a skillet for 5-6 minutes.

2 cups/500 mL whipping cream

Add cream to skillet and stir until blended with the vegetables. Slowly bring cream to a boil.

salt
freshly ground black pepper

Season with salt and pepper to taste.

Add fettuccine to sauce in skillet. Toss and heat.

1/4 cup/50 mL Parmesan cheese, freshly grated

Add Parmesan cheese to fettuccine. Toss and heat.

1/4 cup/50 mL Parmesan cheese, freshly grated
1 tbsp./15 mL fresh parsley, finely chopped

Put fettuccine on a warm serving platter or warm plates. Sprinkle with Parmesan cheese and chopped fresh parsley and serve.

Fusilli

Fusilli—corkscrew shaped spiral pasta—pasta that appears to have been twisted on a spindle—the same shape as rotini, only smaller and finer.

Fusilli al Prosciutto

Fusilli with Prosciutto, Grated Hardboiled Eggs, Nutmeg and Parsley

Cook 1 lb./500 g fusilli al dente: 3-5 minutes for fresh fusilli; 5-7 minutes for packaged fusilli (to cook pasta, see p. 15).

Sauce:

1/8 lb./50 g prosciutto, julienned 1 tbsp./15 mL unsalted butter 1 tbsp./15 mL olive oil	*Sauté prosciutto in butter and olive oil in a skillet for approximately 1 minute.*
1 cup/250 mL whipping cream	*Add cream to skillet and simmer for 2-3 minutes until sauce thickens slightly.*
1/2 cup/125 mL chicken consommé (see p. 21) 2 tbsp./25 mL unsalted butter	*Add chicken consommé and butter to skillet and stir until well blended. Simmer until sauce is smooth and velvety.*
salt freshly ground black pepper 1/4 tsp./1 mL ground nutmeg 1 tbsp./15 mL fresh parsley, finely chopped	*Season with salt, pepper, nutmeg and parsley.*
3 hardboiled eggs, grated (reserving 2 tbsp./25 mL grated hardboiled egg for garnish)	*Add grated hardboiled egg to skillet and gently stir.*
	Add fusilli to sauce in skillet. Toss and heat.
4-6 tbsp./60-90 mL Parmesan cheese, freshly grated	*Add Parmesan cheese to fusilli. Toss and heat.*
2 tbsp./25 mL grated hardboiled egg (reserved above) 1 tbsp./15 mL fresh parsley, finely chopped	*Put fusilli on a warm serving platter or warm plates. Sprinkle with grated hardboiled egg and chopped fresh parsley and serve.*

Fusilli alla Caruso

Fussilli with Eggplant

Cook 1 lb./500 g fusilli al dente: 3-5 minutes for fresh fusilli; 5-7 minutes for packaged fusilli (to cook pasta, see p. 15).

Sauce:

3 large eggplants salt	*Cut tops and bottoms off eggplant. Stand eggplant upright and cut down the four sides of each eggplant, leaving a square centre behind. Discard centres. Put side wedges of eggplant, skin side down, on paper towels on a tray and sprinkle with salt to draw the water and bitterness out of the eggplant. Let eggplant sit for 30 minutes, then rinse and cube.*

3 whole cloves garlic 3 tbsp./50 mL olive oil	*Sauté garlic in olive oil in a skillet until light brown. Remove garlic from skillet.*
	Add eggplant to skillet and sauté for 5 minutes, stirring frequently.
1/2 cup/125 mL dry white wine	*Add white wine to skillet and reduce by simmering for 2-3 minutes.*
1 (28 oz./796 mL) can of Italian tomatoes, and liquid 1 stalk celery, chopped	*Put tomatoes, tomato liquid and celery together in a blender or food processor and purée.*
	Add puréed tomato mixture to skillet and cook for approximately 15 minutes.
salt white pepper	*Season with salt and pepper to taste.*
	Add fusilli to sauce in skillet. Toss and heat.
2 tbsp./25 mL Parmesan cheese, freshly grated 10 leaves of fresh basil, julienned	*Put fusilli on a warm serving platter or warm plates. Sprinkle with Parmesan cheese and julienned fresh basil and serve.*

Fusilli alla Giudea

Serves 4-6

Fusilli with Artichokes and Sage

Cook fusilli al dente: 3-5 minutes for fresh fusilli; 5-7 minutes for packaged fusilli (to cook pasta, see p. 15).

Sauce:

4 medium fresh artichokes, stemmed, with the spiky tips trimmed and any brown outer leaves discarded — or 1 (14 oz./398 mL) can artichoke hearts, drained, reserving the liquid juice of 1/2 lemon chicken consommé (see p. 21) (to cover 3/4) 3 tbsp./50 mL olive oil 1/4 tsp./1 mL fresh oregano, finely chopped 3 leaves of fresh sage, finely chopped juice of 1/2 lemon	*Squeeze lemon juice over tops and bottoms of artichokes, then stand them upright in a stainless steel or enamel saucepan large enough to contain them. Cover artichokes three-quarters with chicken consommé. Add olive oil, oregano, sage and lemon juice to saucepan. Bring consommé to a boil and cook artichokes for 15 minutes until they are tender, but firm. Drain pot and reserve the liquid. Rinse artichokes and allow them to cool. When artichokes are cool, halve them. Clean artichokes of spiny parts and hair. Cut artichokes in wedges with the leaves attached. If using canned artichoke hearts, heat as above, but only for 5 minutes, and cut in wedges.*
1 whole clove garlic 2 tbsp./25 mL olive oil	*Sauté artichoke wedges and garlic in olive oil in a skillet for 1-2 minutes.*
1/3 cup/75 mL dry white wine	*Add white wine to skillet and reduce by simmering for approximately 2 minutes.*

(cont'd over)

	Add artichoke liquid to skillet and simmer for 2 minutes more. Remove garlic from skillet.
3 tbsp./50 mL unsalted butter	Add butter to skillet and blend in.
1 firm, ripe tomato, seeded and julienned	Add tomato to skillet and simmer for 1-2 minutes.
salt freshly ground black pepper	Season with salt and pepper to taste.
	Add fusilli to sauce in skillet. Toss and heat.
1 tbsp./15 mL Parmesan cheese, freshly grated 4 tsp./20 mL tomato, concassé 4-6 sprigs of fresh basil	Put fusilli on a warm serving platter or warm plates. Sprinkle with Parmesan cheese. Garnish with tomato concassé and sprigs of fresh basil and serve.

Fusilli con Gamberetti

Serves 4-6

Fusilli with Shrimp and Cream

Cook 1 lb./500 g fusilli al dente: 3-5 minutes for fresh fusilli; 5-7 minutes for packaged fusilli (to cook pasta, see p. 15).

Sauce:

2 tbsp./25 mL shallot, finely chopped 2 tbsp./25 mL unsalted butter	Sauté shallot in butter in a skillet for 1 minute until soft and transparent.
1/2 lb./250 g fresh shrimp, peeled and cleaned — or 1/2 lb./250 g individually quick frozen shrimp, defrosted	Add shrimp to skillet and quickly toss for 1 minute.
2 tbsp./25 mL brandy	Add brandy to skillet and flambé.
1/4 cup/50 mL dry white wine	Add white wine to skillet and reduce by simmering for 1-2 minutes.
1 cup/250 mL whipping cream	Add cream to skillet and stir until well blended. Simmer for 2-3 minutes until sauce thickens slightly.
2 tbsp./25 mL unsalted butter	Add butter to sauce and blend in. Cook until sauce is thick and velvety.
salt freshly ground black pepper	Season with salt and pepper to taste.
	Add fusilli to sauce in skillet. Toss and heat.
1/4 cup/50 mL Parmesan cheese, freshly grated 1 tbsp./15 mL fresh parsley, finely chopped	Put fusilli on a warm serving platter or warm plates. Sprinkle with Parmesan cheese and chopped fresh parsley and serve.

Fusilli con Salsa Capesante

Fusilli with Scallop Sauce

Cook 1 lb./500 g fusilli al dente: 3-5 minutes for fresh fusilli; 5-7 minutes for packaged fusilli (to cook pasta, see p. 15).

Sauce:

1/4 lb./125 g fresh scallops, with the orange coral attached (reserving the orange coral for garnish) 1 shallot, finely chopped 1 stalk celery, chopped 1 cup/250 mL dry white wine	*Simmer scallops, shallot and celery in white wine in a saucepan until wine has reduced by one-half.*
	Put contents of saucepan in a blender or food processor and purée. Pour puréed scallop mixture into a skillet.
1 cup/250 mL fish consommé (see p. 20) or nectar	*Add fish stock or clam nectar a little at a time to skillet and stir until well blended. Simmer until sauce is smooth and velvety.*
salt white pepper	*Season with salt and pepper to taste.*
	Add fusilli to sauce in skillet. Toss and heat.
2 tbsp./25 mL fresh parsley, finely chopped orange coral from scallops (reserved above)	*Put fusilli on a warm serving platter or warm plates. Sprinkle with chopped fresh parsley. Garnish with orange coral from scallops and serve.*

Fusilli Lombardi

Fusilli with Gorgonzola Cheese

Cook 1 lb./500 g fusilli al dente: 3-5 minutes for fresh fusilli; 5-7 minutes for packaged fusilli (to cook pasta, see p. 15).

Sauce:

1 cup/250 mL Gorgonzola cheese — at room temperature (reserving 1/2 cup/125 mL Gorgonzola cheese for garnish) 1 1/2 cups/375 mL whipping cream 2 tbsp./25 mL dry sherry	*Mix Gorgonzola cheese, cream and sherry together in a bowl. Set aside.*

(cont'd over)

Illustration #3 (page 51): Fettuccine con Prosciutto e Piselli/Fettuccine with Prosciutto and Peas photographed against Rosso Levanto marble, courtesy of Quadra Stone Company Ltd.; bowl courtesy of Umberto's Restaurants Ltd.
Illustration #4 (page 52): Fusilli alla Giudea/Fusilli with Artichokes and Sage photographed against Duchess Rose marble, courtesy of Quadra Stone Company Ltd.; plate courtesy of Umberto's Restaurants Ltd.

1/4 cup/50 mL chicken consommé (see p. 21) 2 tbsp./25 mL dry white wine 2 tbsp./25 mL unsalted butter	*Mix chicken consommé, white wine and butter together in a skillet and bring to a boil.*
	Reduce heat in skillet and add Gorgonzola cheese mixture. Stir until well blended and cook for approximately 3 minutes until sauce thickens slightly.
salt freshly ground black pepper	*Season with salt and pepper to taste.*
	Add fusilli to sauce in skillet. Toss and heat.
1/2 cup/125 mL Gorgonzola cheese (reserved above) 1 tbsp./15 mL fresh parsley, finely chopped	*Put fusilli on a warm serving platter or warm plates. Crumble Gorgonzola cheese over top of fusilli. Sprinkle with chopped fresh parsley and serve.*

usilli Romana

Serves 4-6

Fusilli with Bacon, Onion and Rosemary

Cook 1 lb./500 g fusilli al dente: 3-5 minutes for fresh fusilli; 5-7 minutes for packaged fusilli (to cook pasta, see p. 15).

Sauce:

8 slices of bacon, julienned	*Fry bacon in a skillet until it is half done.*
1/4 of 1 medium white onion, julienned	*Add onion to skillet and continue to fry bacon until it is crisp. Drain bacon fat.*
1 tsp./5 mL leaves of fresh rosemary	*Add rosemary to skillet to flavour.*
1/2 cup/125 mL chicken consommé (see p. 21) 2 tbsp./25 mL unsalted butter	*Add chicken consommé and butter to skillet and simmer for approximately 2 minutes.*
salt freshly ground black pepper	*Season with salt and pepper to taste.*
	Add fusilli to sauce in skillet. Toss and heat.
4-6 tbsp./60-90 mL Parmesan cheese, freshly grated	*Add Parmesan cheese to fusilli. Toss and heat.*
1 tbsp./15 mL tomato, concassé 4-6 sprigs of fresh rosemary	*Put fusilli on a warm serving platter or warm plates. Garnish with tomato concassé and sprigs of fresh rosemary and serve.*

Gnocchi

Gnocchi—"potato dumplings"—pasta made with potato and flour rather than egg and flour, then rolled, cut and pinched.

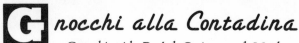nocchi alla Contadina

Gnocchi with Puréed Onions and Mushrooms and Toasted Almonds

2 1/2 lbs./1.25 kg potatoes, washed and peeled cold water (to cover)	Boil potatoes in water in a pot for 30-45 minutes until tender, then drain. Put potatoes through a mouli, a ricer or a food grinder into a bowl. Set aside and keep warm.
2/3 cup/150 mL flour 2 egg yolks 2 tsp./10 mL salt 1/4 tsp./1 mL white pepper	Lightly flour a clean cutting board. Make a well of flour. Add egg yolks and salt and pepper to well, then gradually add still warm mashed potatoes and mix together with your hands or with two forks until potatoes are used up and a firm-textured dough is formed. Set dough aside and clean cutting board. Lightly flour cutting board once again. Take one-quarter of the dough and roll out until 1 inch/2.5 cm in diameter. Cut dough with a knife into 1/2 inch/1 cm pieces and pinch to make gnocchi. Lightly flour a tray and set gnocchi on tray. Repeat until all the dough is used up.
salt cold water	Add salt to water in a pot. Bring water to a boil on high heat and drop gnocchi, a few at a time, into boiling water. When gnocchi float to the surface, they are done. This should take approximately 3 mintues. Remove gnocchi from pot with a spider strainer or slotted spoon. Drain gnocchi and put on a warm serving platter. Set aside.

Sauce:

1/2 of 1 medium white onion, finely chopped 1 tbsp./15 mL unsalted butter 1 tbsp./15 mL vegetable oil	Sauté onion in butter and vegetable oil in a skillet for 1 minute until soft and transparent.
1 lb./500 g fresh mushrooms, cleaned and sliced	Add mushrooms to skillet and stir fry for approximately 2 minutes.
1/3 cup/75 mL dry white wine juice of 1/2 lemon	Add white wine and lemon juice to skillet and reduce by simmering for approximately 3 minutes.
	Put contents of skillet in a blender or food processor and purée. Return puréed onion and mushroom mixture to skillet.
1 1/2 cups/375 mL whipping cream	Add cream to skillet and stir until well blended. Simmer for approximately 3 minutes until sauce thickens slightly.

2 tbsp./25 mL unsalted butter whipping cream (optional)	Add butter to sauce in skillet and blend in. Cook until sauce is smooth and velvety. (If sauce is too thick, add more cream.)
salt white pepper	Season with salt and pepper to taste.
2 tbsp./25 mL sliced almonds, toasted 1 tbsp./15 mL fresh parsley, finely chopped	Pour sauce over gnocchi on warm serving platter. Sprinkle with toasted sliced almonds and chopped fresh parsley. Serve on warm serving platter or warm plates.

Gnocchi Piemontese

Serves 4-6

Gnocchi with Meat Sauce

2 1/2 lbs./1.25 kg potatoes, washed and peeled cold water (to cover)	Boil potatoes in water in a pot for 30-45 minutes until tender, then drain. Put potatoes through a mouli, a ricer or a food grinder into a bowl. Set aside and keep warm.
2/3 cup/150 mL flour 2 egg yolks 2 tsp./10 mL salt 1/4 tsp./1 mL white pepper	Lightly flour a clean cutting board. Make a well of flour. Add egg yolks and salt and pepper to well, then gradually add still warm mashed potatoes and mix together with your hands or with two forks until potatoes are used up and a firm-textured dough is formed. Set dough aside and clean cutting board. Lightly flour cutting board once again. Take one-quarter of the dough and roll out until 1 inch/2.5 cm in diameter. Cut dough with a knife into 1/2 inch/1 cm pieces and pinch to make gnocchi. Lightly flour a tray and set gnocchi on tray. Repeat until all the dough is used up.
salt cold water	Add salt to water in a pot. Bring water to a boil on high heat and drop gnocchi, a few at a time, into boiling water. When gnocchi float to the surface, they are done. This should take approximately 3 minutes. Remove gnocchi from pot with a spider strainer or slotted spoon. Drain gnocchi and put on a warm platter.
	Pre-heat oven to 350°F/180°C.
1 tbsp./15 mL unsalted butter 3 cups/750 mL meat sauce (see p. 18) 1/4 cup/50 mL Parmesan cheese, freshly grated	Butter the bottom of a casserole dish. Put a layer of gnocchi in bottom of casserole dish. Put a layer of meat sauce on top of gnocchi. Repeat with layers of gnocchi and meat sauce until gnocchi are used up. Sprinkle with Parmesan cheese on top.
	Put casserole dish in oven at 350°F/180°C and bake for 5 minutes. Serve in casserole dish.

Lasagna

Lasagna—pasta made by layering 5 x 3 inch/12.5 x 8 cm cooked fresh pasta squares (or packaged lasagna noodles) with stuffing between the layers, then baking in a pan in the oven for 30 minutes.

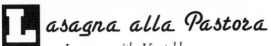# Lasagna alla Pastora

Lasagna with Vegetables

Cook 1 lb./500 g lasagna noodles (or 1 1/2 lbs./700 g lasagna noodles, if using packaged lasagna) al dente: 3-5 minutes for fresh lasagna noodles; 5-7 minutes for packaged lasagna noodles (to cook pasta, see p. 15).

1 large eggplant, thinly sliced 1 tbsp./15 mL unsalted butter 2 tbsp./25 mL olive oil	*Sauté eggplant in butter and oil in a skillet for 1-2 minutes. Drain eggplant on a paper towel on a tray. Do not stack.*
4 medium zucchini, thinly sliced flour (to dust)	*Lightly flour zucchini, shaking off the excess. Add zucchini to skillet and sauté both sides very quickly for approximately 30 seconds per side. Add more butter and oil, if necessary. Drain zucchini on a paper towel on a tray. Do not stack.*
	Pre-heat oven to 350°F/180°C.
2 tbsp./25 mL unsalted butter 3 cups/750 mL tomato sauce (see p. 19) 3 cups/750 mL Béchamel sauce (see p. 18) 1 1/2 cups/375 mL Parmesan cheese, freshly grated	*Butter the bottom of a 16x12x3 inch/ 40x30x8 cm pan. Put a layer of lasagna noodles in pan. Spread a layer of eggplant and zucchini on top of noodles. Put a thin layer of tomato sauce and Béchamel sauce on top of eggplant and zucchini. Sprinkle with a layer of Parmesan cheese. Repeat for three layers, ending with a layer of noodles on top.*
1/4 cup/50 mL Parmesan cheese, freshly grated 2 tbsp./25 mL fresh parsley, finely chopped	*Put pan in oven at 350°F/180°C and bake for 30 minutes. Remove pan from oven and allow lasagna to sit for 5 minutes to firm up before serving. Cut with a knife into 4x5 inch/ 10x12.5 cm portions and serve on warm plates. Sprinkle with Parmesan cheese and chopped fresh parsley.*

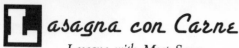# Lasagna con Carne

Serves 6-8

Lasagna with Meat Sauce

Cook 1 lb./500 g lasagna noodles (or 1 1/2 lbs./700 g lasagna noodles, if using packaged lasagna) al dente: 3-5 minutes for fresh lasagna noodles; 5-7 minutes for packaged lasagna noodles (to cook pasta, see p. 15).

Pre-heat oven to 350°F/180°C.

2 tbsp./25 mL unsalted butter 1/4 cup/50 mL Béchamel sauce (see p. 18) 4 cups/1 L meat sauce (see p. 18) 2 cups/500 mL Béchamel sauce (see p. 18) 2 cups/500 mL Parmesan cheese, freshly grated	*Butter the bottom of a 16x12x3 inch/ 40x30x8 cm pan. Put a thin layer of Béchamel sauce in pan. Put a layer of noodles on top of Béchamel sauce. Spread a layer of meat sauce on top of noodles. Put a layer of Béchamel sauce on top of meat sauce. Sprinkle with a layer of Parmesan cheese. Repeat for three layers, ending with a layer of noodles on top.*

Put pan in oven at 350°F/180°C and bake for 30 minutes. Remove pan from oven and allow lasagna to sit for 5 minutes to firm up before serving. Cut with a knife into 4x5 inch/ 10x12.5 cm portions and serve on warm plates.

Lasagna Lido di Venezia

Serves 6-8

Lasagna with Seafood

Cook 1 lb./500 g lasagna noodles (or 1 1/2 lbs./700 g lasagna noodles, if using packaged lasagna) al dente: 3-5 minutes for fresh lasagna noodles; 5-7 minutes for packaged lasagna noodles (to cook pasta, see p. 15).

1 lb./500 g squid	*Clean squid by pulling off the head and pulling out the entrails. Lay squid on a cutting board or flat surface and, using a sharp knife, scrape the skin off. Wash squid thoroughly in cold running water. Cut off tentacles and make sure that the beak-like mouth is discarded. Chop tentacles and body in 1/2 inch/1 cm pieces. Pat squid dry with a cloth or paper towel. Set aside.*
1/2 of 1 medium white onion, thinly sliced 1 tbsp./15 mL unsalted butter 1 tbsp./15 mL olive oil	*Sauté onion in butter and olive oil in a skillet for 1 minute until soft and transparent.*
	Add squid to skillet and sauté for 2-3 minutes.

1 lb./500 g fillet of fresh salmon, julienned	*Add salmon, red snapper, scallops and shrimp to skillet and sauté for 3-4 minutes until fish is done and still moist.*
1 lb./500 g fillet of fresh red snapper, julienned	
1/2 lb./250 g fresh scallops, thinly sliced, if large	
3/4 lb./350 g fresh baby shrimp, peeled and cleaned	
1/2 cup/125 mL dry white wine	*Add white wine to skillet and reduce by simmering for 1-2 minutes.*
2 cups/500 mL Béchamel sauce (see p. 18)	*Add Béchamel sauce to seafood in skillet and gently mix together. Simmer for approximately 2 minutes.*
	Pre-heat oven to 350°F/180°C.
2 tbsp./25 mL unsalted butter 1 cup/250 mL Béchamel sauce (see p. 18)	*Butter the bottom of a 16x12x3 inch/ 40x30x8 cm pan. Put a layer of lasagna noodles in pan. Spread a layer of the seafood mixture on top of noodles. Repeat for three layers, ending with a layer of noodles and Béchamel sauce on top.*
4-6 scallions, washed and cleaned, then julienned lengthwise	*Put pan in oven at 350°F/180°C and bake for 30 minutes. Remove pan from oven and allow lasagna to sit for 5 minutes to firm up before serving. Cut with a knife into 4x5 inch/ 10x12.5 cm portions and serve on warm plates. Garnish with julienned scallions.*

Lasagna Marchigiana

Serves 6-8

Lasagna with Eggplant, Meat Sauce and Goat Cheese

Cook 1 lb./500 g lasagna noodles (or 1 1/2 lbs./700 g lasagna noodles, if using packaged lasagna) al dente: 3-5 minutes for fresh lasagna noodles; 5-7 minutes for packaged lasagna noodles (to cook pasta, see p. 15). Try this with beet noodles.

3 medium eggplants salt	*Cut tops and bottoms off eggplant. Slice eggplant in rounds 1/4 inch/.5 cm thick. Put eggplant rounds on paper towels on a tray and sprinkle with salt to draw the water and bitterness out of the eggplant. Let eggplant sit for 30 minutes, then rinse.*
vegetable oil	*Put oil in a skillet to half the depth of skillet. Heat oil. When oil is hot, fry eggplant in oil in skillet for 1-2 minutes. Put fried eggplant in one layer on a paper towel on a tray and pat dry. Do not stack eggplant. Make sure that eggplant*

(cont'd over)

61

is well drained of oil before continuing with recipe.

Pre-heat oven to 350°F/180°C.

2 tbsp./25 mL unsalted butter	*Butter the bottom of a 16x12x3 inch/*
2 cups/500 mL meat sauce (see p. 18)	*40x30x8 cm pan. Put a layer of lasagna noodles in pan. Spread a layer of meat sauce on*
1 cup/250 mL Béchamel sauce (see p. 18)	*top of noodles. Put a thin layer of Béchamel sauce on top of meat sauce. Cover with a layer*
3/4 lb./350 g goat cheese	*of eggplant. Crumble goat cheese on top of*
1/2 cup/125 mL Béchamel sauce (see p. 18)	*eggplant. Repeat with a layer of noodles, a layer of meat sauce, a thin layer of Béchamel sauce, a*
1/2 cup/125 mL Parmesan cheese, freshly grated	*layer of eggplant, and goat cheese on top of eggplant. End with a layer of noodles and Béchamel sauce on top. Sprinkle with Parmesan cheese.*

Put pan in oven at 350°F/180°C and bake for 30 minutes. Remove pan from oven and allow lasagna to sit for 5 minutes to firm up before serving. Cut with a knife into 4x5 inch/ 10x12.5 cm portions and serve on warm plates.

Lasagna Verde alla Greca

Serves 6-8

Lasagna with Assorted Mushrooms and Feta Cheese

Cook 1 lb./500 g spinach lasagna noodles (or 1 1/2 lbs./700 g spinach lasagna noodles, if using packaged lasagna) al dente: 3-5 minutes for fresh lasagna noodles; 5-7 minutes for packaged lasagna noodles (to cook pasta, see p. 15).

3 shallots, finely chopped	*Sauté shallots in butter in a skillet for 1 minute*
2 tbsp./25 mL unsalted butter	*until soft and transparent.*
3 medium cloves garlic, finely chopped	*Add garlic and mushrooms to skillet and sauté for approximately 4 minutes until mushrooms*
1 cup/250 mL fresh Chanterelle mushrooms, cleaned and sliced	*are lightly browned.*
1 cup/250 mL fresh Cèpes mushrooms, cleaned and sliced	
1 cup/250 mL fresh Oyster mushrooms, cleaned and sliced	
2 cups/500 mL fresh champignon mushrooms, cleaned and sliced	
1/2 cup/125 mL dry white wine	*Add white wine to skillet and reduce by simmering for 1 minute.*
2 cups/500 mL whipping cream	*Add cream to skillet and stir until well blended. Reduce by simmering until sauce thickens slightly.*

salt white pepper 8 leaves of fresh basil, julienned 1/4 tsp./1 mL fresh thyme, finely chopped 1/4 tsp./1 mL fresh marjoram, finely chopped	*Season with salt, pepper, basil, thyme and marjoram.*
2 cups/500 mL Béchamel sauce (see p. 18)	*Add Béchamel sauce to mushroom sauce in skillet and stir until well blended. Simmer for approximately 2 minutes.* *Pre-heat oven to 350°F/180°C.*
2 tbsp./25 mL unsalted butter 2 cups/500 mL Feta cheese 1/4 tsp./1 mL lemon zest 1 cup/250 mL Béchamel sauce (see p. 18)	*Butter the bottom of a 16x12x3 inch/ 40x30x8 cm pan. Put a layer of lasagna noodles in pan. Spread a layer of Béchamel-mushroom sauce mixture on top of noodles. Put another layer of noodles, then crumble one-half of the Feta cheese on top of noodles. Add lemon zest to Feta cheese. Repeat with a layer of noodles, a layer of Béchamel-mushroom sauce, a layer of noodles and the other half of the Feta cheese. End with a layer of noodles and Béchamel sauce on top.*
4-6 sprigs of fresh basil	*Put pan in oven at 350°F/180°C and bake for 30 minutes. Remove pan from oven and allow lasagna to sit for 5 minutes to firm up before serving. Cut with a knife into 4x5 inch/ 10x12.5 cm portions and serve on warm plates. Garnish with sprigs of fresh basil.*

Linguine

Linguine—"little tongues"—pasta that is halfway between a thin, flat ribbon and a cylindrical strand—like spaghetti, only flatter and broader.

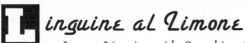
Linguine al Limone

Serves 4-6

Lemon Linguine with Stracchino Cheese, Avocado, Shrimp and Parsley

Add lemon juice to the flour and eggs when you're making the pasta (to make fresh pasta, see p. 10) or use packaged linguine and sprinkle with lemon zest at the end. Cook 1 lb./500 g linguine al dente: approximately 1 minute for fresh lemon linguine that you've just made; 5-7 minutes for packaged linguine (to cook pasta, see p. 15).

Sauce:

1/2 cup/125 mL whipping cream 1/2 cup/125 mL Stracchino cheese, freshly grated	*Mix cream and Stracchino cheese together in a skillet and simmer for 3-4 minutes until cheese has melted.*
1 cup/250 mL fresh shrimp, peeled and cleaned	*Add shrimp to skillet and simmer for approximately 2 minutes until sauce is smooth and velvety.*
salt freshly ground black pepper	*Season with salt and pepper to taste.*
	Add lemon linguine to sauce in skillet. Toss and heat.
1 medium avocado, peeled, cored and cut in chunks	*Put avocado on top of linguine and toss.*
1 tbsp./15 mL fresh parsley, finely chopped lemon zest (optional)	*Put linguine on a warm serving platter or warm plates. Sprinkle with chopped fresh parsley and serve. If using packaged linguine, sprinkle with lemon zest at end and serve.*

Linguine al Pesto

Serves 4-6

Linguine with Pesto Sauce

Cook 1 lb./500 g linguine al dente: 3-5 minutes for fresh linguine; 5-7 minutes for packaged linguine (to cook pasta, see p. 15).

Sauce:

2 cups/500 mL fresh basil, stem and leaves, packed in a measuring cup 1/4 lb./125 g pine nuts 2 medium cloves garlic 1/2 cup/125 mL Parmesan cheese, freshly grated 1/4 cup/50 mL Romano cheese, freshly grated 1/2 cup/125 mL olive oil 2 tbsp./25 mL unsalted butter (optional) 1/8 tsp./pinch of salt	*Put basil, pine nuts, garlic, Parmesan cheese, Romano cheese, olive oil, butter and salt in a blender or food processor and mix together thoroughly, then put mixture in a skillet.*

(cont'd over)

1/2 cup/125 mL chicken consommé (see p. 21) 1 tbsp./15 mL unsalted butter	*Add chicken consommé and butter to skillet and stir until well blended. Simmer for approximately 5 minutes.*
	Add linguine to sauce in skillet. Toss and heat.
1/2 cup/125 mL Parmesan cheese, freshly grated 4-6 sprigs of fresh basil	*Put linguine on a warm serving platter or warm plates. Sprinkle with Parmesan cheese. Garnish with sprigs of fresh basil and serve.*

L inguine alle Vongole

Serves 4-6

Linguine with Clam Sauce

Cook 1 lb./500 g linguine al dente: 3-5 minutes for fresh linguine; 5-7 minutes for packaged linguine (to cook pasta, see p. 15).

Sauce:

1/2 cup/125 mL white onion, finely diced 1 tsp./5 mL garlic, finely chopped 2 tbsp./25 mL unsalted butter	*Sauté onion and garlic in butter in a skillet for 1-2 minutes until onion is soft and transparent. Set aside.*
1 cup/250 mL cold water 1/2 cup/125 mL dry white wine 1 bay leaf	*Put water, white wine and bay leaf in a pot and bring to a boil.*
6 lbs./3 kg fresh clams, washed and cleaned, or 2 (5 oz./142 g) cans clams, reserving the liquid	*Add onion and garlic to pot and stir. Add clams to pot, then cover pot and steam clams for 5-6 minutes until their shells open. Remove clams from pot and set aside. Let liquid in pot settle, then drain pot, reserving 1/2 cup/125 mL liquid in bottom of pot. Strain liquid through a sieve lined with a linen or muslin cloth into a bowl. Set aside. Remove clams from shells, reserving 16-24 clams in shells for garnish.*
5 tbsp./75 mL unsalted butter 1 1/2 tsp./7 mL garlic, finely chopped 3 tbsp./50 mL fresh parsley, finely chopped	*Put clams, clam liquid, butter, garlic and parsley together in a skillet and simmer for approximately 4 minutes.*
1/3 cup/75 mL dry white wine	*Add white wine to skillet and reduce by simmering for approximately 2 minutes.*
salt freshly ground black pepper	*Season with salt and pepper to taste. (Be careful with the salt as clams may be salty to begin with.)*
	Add linguine to sauce in skillet. Toss and heat.
16-24 steamed clams, in shells (reserved above)	*Put linguine on a warm serving platter or warm plates. Garnish with clams in the shell and serve. Cheese not recommended.*

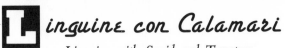

Linguine con Calamari

Linguine with Squid and Tomatoes

Serves 4-6

Cook 1 lb./500 g linguine al dente: 3-5 minutes for fresh linguine; 5-7 minutes for packaged linguine (to cook pasta, see p. 15).

Sauce:

1 lb./500 g squid salt freshly ground black pepper juice of 1/2 lemon 2 tbsp./25 mL unsalted butter 2 tbsp./25 mL olive oil	*Clean squid by pulling off the head and pulling out the entrails. Lay squid on a cutting board or flat surface and, using a sharp knife, scrape the skin off. Wash squid thoroughly in cold running water. Cut off tentacles and make sure that the beak-like mouth is discarded. Chop tentacles and body in 1/4 inch/.5 cm pieces. Pat squid dry with a cloth or paper towel. Season squid with salt, pepper and lemon juice. Sauté squid in butter and olive oil in a skillet for 2-3 minutes until golden.*
1/4 cup/50 mL dry white wine	*Add white wine to skillet and reduce by simmering for 1-2 minutes.*
1 1/2 cups/375 mL tomato sauce (see p. 19)	*Add tomato sauce to skillet and simmer for approximately 3 minutes.*
salt freshly ground black pepper	*Adjust seasoning with salt and pepper to taste.*
	Add linguine to sauce in skillet. Toss and heat.
1 tsp./5 mL fresh parsley, finely chopped	*Put linguine on a warm serving platter or warm plates. Sprinkle with chopped fresh parsley and serve. Cheese not recommended.*

Linguine con Cozze

Linguine with Mussels

Serves 4-6

Cook 1 lb./500 g linguine al dente: 3-5 minutes for fresh linguine; 5-7 minutes for packaged linguine (to cook pasta, see p. 15).

Sauce:

1/2 cup/125 mL white onion, finely diced 1 tsp./5 mL garlic, finely chopped 2 tbsp./25 mL unsalted butter	*Sauté onion and garlic in butter in a skillet for 1-2 minutes until shallots are soft and transparent. Set aside.*
1 cup/250 mL cold water 1/2 cup/125 mL dry white wine	*Put water and white wine in a pot and bring to a boil.*
4 1/2 lbs./2.25 kg black mussels, washed and cleaned	*Add onion and garlic to pot and stir. Add mussels to pot, then cover pot and steam mussels*

(cont'd over)

for 3-4 minutes until their shells open. Remove mussels from pot and set aside. Drain pot, reserving 1/2 cup/125 mL liquid. Strain liquid through a sieve lined with a linen or muslin cloth into a bowl. Set aside. Remove mussels from shells, reserving 8-12 mussels in shells for garnish. Set aside.

2 shallots, finely chopped
2 cloves garlic, finely chopped
2 tbsp./25 mL unsalted butter

Sauté shallots and garlic in butter in a skillet for 1-2 minutes until shallots are soft and transparent.

Add mussels to skillet and simmer for 2-3 minutes.

3/4 cup/175 mL tomato sauce
(see p. 19)

Add tomato sauce, mussel liquid and parsley to skillet and simmer for 2-3 minutes.

salt
freshly ground black pepper

Season with salt and pepper to taste. (Be careful with the salt as mussels may be salty to begin with.)

Add linguine to sauce in skillet. Toss and heat.

8-12 steamed black mussels, in shells
(reserved above)

Put linguine on a warm serving platter or warm plates. Garnish with mussels in the shell and serve. Cheese not recommended.

L inguine con Salciccia
Serves 4-6

Linguine with Italian Sausage

Cook 1 lb./500 g linguine al dente: 3-5 minutes for fresh linguine; 5-7 minutes for packaged linguine (to cook pasta, see p. 15).

3/4 lb./350 g Italian sausage,
3 tbsp./50 mL olive oil

Sauté whole sausage in olive oil in a skillet for 2-3 minutes, then thinly slice and return to skillet.

1/2 tsp./2 mL hot red chili pepper,
finely chopped
12 whole leaves of fresh basil

Add chili pepper and basil to skillet and simmer for approximately 2 minutes.

salt
freshly ground black pepper

Season with salt and pepper to taste. (Be careful with the seasoning as sausage are already seasoned and you have added hot red chili pepper to the skillet.)

Add linguine to skillet. Toss and heat.

4-6 tbsp./60-90 mL Parmesan cheese,
freshly grated
1 tbsp./15 mL fresh parsley,
finely chopped

Put linguine on a warm serving platter or warm plates. Sprinkle with Parmesan cheese and chopped fresh parsley and serve.

Linguine Cetriolate

Serves 4-6

Linguine with Cucumber and Dill

Cook 1 lb./500 g linguine al dente: 3-5 minutes for fresh linguine; 5-7 minutes for packaged linguine (to cook pasta, see p. 15).

Sauce:

1 shallot, finely chopped 1 tbsp./15 mL unsalted butter	*Sauté shallot in butter in a skillet for 1 minute until soft and transparent.*
1 medium cucumber, peeled and thinly sliced 2 tsp./10 mL fresh dill, finely chopped	*Add cucumber and dill to skillet and sauté for approximately 2 minutes.*
1/4 cup/50 mL chicken consommé (see p. 21)	*Add chicken consommé to skillet and simmer for approximately 3 minutes.*
salt white pepper	*Season with salt and pepper to taste.*
	Add linguine to sauce in skillet. Toss and heat.
4-6 tbsp./60-90 mL Parmesan cheese, freshly grated 2 tsp./10 mL tomato, concassé 4-6 sprigs of fresh dill	*Put linguine on a warm serving platter or warm plates. Sprinkle with Parmesan cheese. Garnish with tomato concassé and sprigs of fresh dill and serve.*

Linguine Norvegese

Serves 4-6

Linguine with Herring and Fennel

Cook 1 lb./500 g linguine al dente: 3-5 minutes for fresh linguine; 5-7 minutes for packaged linguine (to cook pasta, see p. 15).

Sauce:

1 small fennel, tip and leaves chopped off (reserving the leaves for garnish), then halved and julienned 2 tbsp./25 mL olive oil	*Sauté fennel in olive oil in a skillet for approximately 3 minutes until soft.*
6 large fresh herring, filleted, scaled and sliced	*Add herring to skillet and sauté for approximately 2 minutes.*
1/4 cup/50 mL dry white wine	*Add white wine to skillet and reduce by simmering for 1-2 minutes.*
salt freshly ground black pepper juice of 1/2 lemon	*Season with salt, pepper and lemon juice.*

(cont'd over)

Illustration #5 (page 69): Linguine con Salciccia/Linguine with Italian Sausage photographed against Violet Moresque marble, courtesy of Quadra Stone Company Ltd.; skillet courtesy of The Salt Box.
Illustration #6 (page 70): Lumache Coltano/Lumache Stuffed with Ricotta Cheese and Chives photographed against Estremoz marble, courtesy of Quadra Stone Company Ltd.; casserole dish courtesy of The Salt Box.

fennel leaves (reserved above), finely chopped
freshly ground black pepper

Add linguine to sauce in skillet. Toss and heat.

Put linguine on a warm serving platter or warm plates. Sprinkle with chopped fresh fennel leaves and freshly ground black pepper and serve.

L inguine Riviera

Serves 4-6

Linguine with Tomatoes and Marjoram

Cook 1 lb./500 g linguine al dente: 3-5 minutes for fresh linguine; 5-7 minutes for packaged linguine (to cook pasta, see p. 15).

Sauce:

6 firm, ripe tomatoes, eyes removed and scored "x" on top

Blanch tomatoes in a pot of boiling water for 20 seconds, then plunge in cold water to stop the cooking. Peel tomatoes, then cut in wedges — approximately 12 wedges per tomato. Set aside.

1/2 of 1 medium sweet white onion, julienned — or 1/2 of 1 medium purple onion, julienned
3 tbsp./50 mL olive oil

Sauté onion in olive oil in a skillet for 1 minute until soft and transparent.

1/4 cup/50 mL chicken consommé (see p. 21)

Add tomatoes and chicken consommé to skillet and cook for approximately 5 minutes.

salt
freshly ground black pepper
1/4 tsp./1 mL garlic, finely chopped
1 1/2 tsp./7 mL fresh marjoram, finely chopped

Season with salt, pepper, garlic and marjoram.

Add linguine to sauce in skillet. Toss and heat.

4-6 tbsp./60-90 mL Parmesan cheese, freshly grated
4-6 sprigs of fresh marjoram

Put linguine on a warm serving platter or warm plates. Sprinkle with Parmesan cheese. Garnish with sprigs of fresh marjoram and serve.

Lumache

Lumache—"snails"—snail shaped pasta—come in small, medium and large; can be stuffed, if large. Not to be confused with *conchiglie*—"conch shells"—which come in a variety of sizes.

Insalata di Lumache

Lumache with Shrimp, a Fillet of Tomatoes, Petits Pois, Anchovies, Lemon Juice, Garlic, Basil and Pure Virgin Olive Oil

This is a recipe for a cold salad. Use the medium size shells. Cook 1 lb./500 g lumache al dente: 3-5 minutes for fresh lumache; 5-7 minutes for packaged lumache (to cook pasta, see p. 15). Drain and rinse. Allow lumache to cool in a bowl.

2-3 firm, ripe tomatoes, eyes removed and scored "x" on top	*Blanch tomatoes in a pot of boiling water for 20 seconds, then plunge in cold water to stop the cooking. Peel, seed and julienne tomatoes. Add tomatoes to lumache in bowl and gently mix together.*
1 cup/250 mL fresh shrimp, peeled and cleaned 1/2 cup/125 mL cooked petits pois 2 fillets of anchovy, washed and mashed	*Add shrimp, petits pois and anchovies to lumache and tomatoes in bowl and gently mix together.*
salt freshly ground black pepper juice of 2 lemons 1/4 tsp./1 mL garlic, finely chopped 8 leaves of fresh basil, julienned	*Season with salt, pepper, lemon juice, garlic and basil. (Be careful with the salt as anchovies are salty to begin with.)*
2/3 cup/150 mL pure virgin olive oil 1/4 cup/50 mL Mozzarella cheese, freshly grated 1 tbsp./15 mL fresh parsley, finely chopped	*Drizzle pure virgin olive oil over top of salad in bowl and gently toss. Sprinkle with Mozzarella cheese and chopped fresh parsley. Serve cold in bowl or put on cold plates and serve.*

Lumache al Modo Mio

Lumache with Zucchini and Pure Virgin Olive Oil

Use the large shells for this recipe. Cook 1 lb./500 g lumache al dente: 3-5 minutes for fresh lumache; 10-15 minutes for packaged lumache (to cook pasta, see p. 15).

4 firm, ripe tomatoes, eyes removed and scored "x" on top	*Blanch tomatoes in a pot of boiling water for 20 seconds, then plunge in cold water to stop the cooking. Peel, seed and chop tomatoes. Put tomatoes in a bowl and set aside.*
4 baby zucchini, washed, with the ends cut off, then thinly sliced cold water (to cover bottom of saucepan)	*Steam zucchini over a saucepan of boiling water until zucchini are done al dente. This should take no longer than 3 minutes. Add zucchini to tomatoes in bowl and gently mix together. (Be careful not to break the zucchini.)*

1 clove garlic, finely chopped 6 leaves of fresh basil, julienned 1 tsp./5 mL fresh oregano, finely chopped	Season with garlic, basil and oregano.
	Put zucchini-tomato mixture in a skillet and heat. Add lumache to skillet. Gently toss and heat.
2 tbsp./25 mL pure virgin olive oil 4-6 tbsp./60-90 mL Parmesan cheese, freshly grated	Put lumache on a warm serving platter or warm plates. Drizzle with pure virgin olive oil. Sprinkle with Parmesan cheese and serve.

 umache di Campagna   Serves 4-6

Lumache Stuffed with Escargot

Use the large shells for this recipe. Cook 1 lb./500 g lumache al dente: 3-5 minutes for fresh lumache; 10-15 minutes for packaged lumache (to cook pasta, see p. 15). Drain and rinse. Allow lumache to cool before stuffing.

Stuffing:

2 shallots, finely chopped 3 tbsp./50 mL unsalted butter	Sauté shallots in butter in a skillet for 1 minute until soft and transparent.
1 (9 oz./250 g) can of escargot, drained and rinsed — 48 escargot 2 medium cloves garlic, finely chopped	Add escargot and garlic to skillet and sauté for approximately 2 minutes.
1/2 cup/125 mL dry white wine	Add white wine to skillet and reduce by simmering for 3-4 minutes.
1 cup/250 mL whipping cream	Add cream to skillet and stir until well blended. Simmer for 2-3 minutes until escargot mixture thickens slightly.
2 tbsp./25 mL unsalted butter 4 tbsp./60 mL pine nuts, toasted 1 tbsp./15 mL fresh parsley, finely chopped zest of 1/2 lemon	Add butter, toasted pine nuts, parsley and lemon zest to skillet and stir until well blended. Simmer until escargot mixture is thick and smooth.
salt freshly grated black pepper	Season with salt and pepper to taste.
	Remove skillet from heat and allow escargot mixture to cool for approximately 5 minutes. Stuff lumache shells with escargot mixture.
	Pre-heat oven to 375°F/190°C.

(cont'd over)

1 tbsp./15 mL unsalted butter 1/4 cup/50 mL whipping cream	Butter the bottom of a casserole dish. Put a thin layer of cream in casserole dish. Put stuffed lumache shells in casserole dish.
3 cups/750 mL Mozzarella cheese, freshly grated	Sprinkle Mozzarella cheese on top of lumache.
4 tbsp./60 mL tomato, concassé 1 1/2 tbsp./20 mL fresh parsley, finely chopped	Put casserole dish in oven at 375°F/190°C and bake for 12-15 minutes. Serve in casserole dish or on warm plates. Garnish with tomato concassé and chopped fresh parsley.

Lumache Coltano

Serves 4-6

Lumache Stuffed with Ricotta Cheese and Chives

Use the large shells for this recipe. Cook 1 lb./500 g lumache al dente: 3-5 minutes for fresh lumache; 10-15 minutes for packaged lumache (to cook pasta, see p. 15). Drain and rinse. Allow lumache to cool before stuffing.

Stuffing:

1 cup/250 mL Ricotta cheese 1/2 cup/125 mL Parmesan cheese, freshly grated 1/4 cup/50 mL Fontina cheese, freshly grated 3 tbsp./50 mL fresh chives, finely chopped 2 egg yolks	Mix Ricotta cheese, Parmesan cheese, Fontina cheese, chives and egg yolks together in a bowl.
	Stuff lumache shells with cheese mixture. Pre-heat oven to 375°F/190°C.
1 tbsp./15 mL unsalted butter 1/4 cup/50 mL whipping cream	Butter the bottom of a casserole dish. Put a thin layer of cream in casserole dish. Put stuffed lumache shells in casserole dish.
3-4 cups/750 mL-1 L tomato sauce (see p. 19) 1/2 cup/125 mL Parmesan cheese, freshly grated	Pour tomato sauce over top of lumache, then sprinkle with Parmesan cheese.
2 tbsp./25 mL fresh chives, finely chopped	Put casserole dish in oven at 375°F/190°C and bake for 15 minutes. Serve in casserole dish or on warm plates. Garnish with chopped fresh chives.

Maccaroni

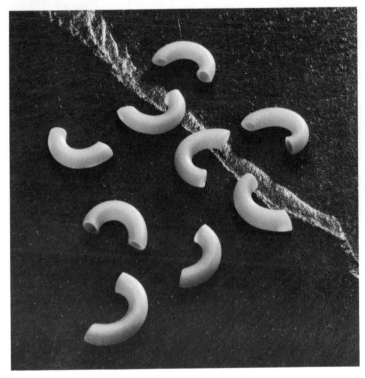

Maccaroni — "macaroni" — this is the generic name for pasta in North America — i.e., all pasta is macaroni. Illustrated above, and the most usual kind, is elbow macaroni.

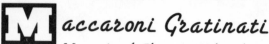 accaroni Gratinati

Serves 4-6

Macaroni and Cheese in Béchamel Sauce with Petits Pois

Cook 1 lb./500 g elbow macaroni al dente: 3-5 minutes for fresh macaroni; 5-7 minutes for packaged macaroni (to cook pasta, see p. 15).

1/2 lb./250 g sharp Cheddar cheese, freshly grated 1/4 cup/50 mL Parmesan cheese, freshly grated 1 cup/250 mL petits pois	*Mix Cheddar cheese, Parmesan cheese and petits pois together in a bowl.*
	Add macaroni to cheese mixture and mix together thoroughly. *Pre-heat oven to 375°F/190°C.*
1 tbsp./15 mL unsalted butter 4 cups/1 L Béchemal sauce (see p. 18) 1/4 cup/50 mL Parmesan cheese, freshly grated 1/4 cup/50 mL fine breadcrumbs	*Butter the bottom of a casserole dish. Put macaroni and cheese mixture in casserole dish. Completely cover macaroni and cheese mixture with Béchamel sauce. (If Béchamel sauce is too thick, add more cream. Sauce should be runny because it thickens when it cooks.) Sprinkle with Parmesan cheese and breadcrumbs on top.* *Put casserole dish in oven at 375°F/190°C and bake for 20 minutes. Serve in casserole dish.*

accaroni con Tacchino

Serves 4-6

Macaroni with Turkey and a Julienne of Onions, Celery and Carrots

Cook 1 lb./500 g elbow macaroni al dente: 3-5 minutes for fresh macaroni; 5-7 minutes for packaged macaroni (to cook pasta, see p. 15).

3/4 lb./350 g cooked breast of turkey, julienned 2 tbsp./25 mL unsalted butter 2 tbsp./25 mL vegetable oil	*Sauté turkey in butter and vegetable oil in a skillet for approximately 2 minutes.*
1/2 of 1 white onion, julienned 2 stalks celery, julienned 1 carrot, julienned	*Add vegetables to skillet and sauté for 3-4 minutes, stirring constantly.*
1 tbsp./15 mL unsalted butter 4 cups/1 L Béchamel sauce (see p. 18) 1/4 cup/50 mL Parmesan cheese, freshly grated 1/4 cup/50 mL fine breadcrumbs	*Butter the bottom of a casserole dish. Put macaroni-turkey-vegetable mixture in casserole dish. Completely cover macaroni-turkey-vegetable mixture with Béchamel sauce. (If Béchamel sauce is too thick, add more cream. Sauce should be runny because it thickens as it cooks.) Sprinkle with Parmesan cheese and breadcrumbs on top.* *Put casserole dish in oven at 375°F/190°C and bake for 15 minutes. Serve in casserole dish.*

Paglia e Fieno

Paglia e Fieno—"straw and hay"—a combination of spinach and egg noodle pasta—most often spinach and egg noodle fettuccine or spinach and egg noodle capelli d'angelo. Illustrated above is spinach and egg noodle fettuccine.

Paglia e Fieno alla Noce

Straw and Hay in a Walnut Sauce

Serves 4-6

Cook 1/2 lb./250 g egg and 1/2 lb./250 g spinach noodles al dente: 3-5 minutes for fresh egg and spinach noodles; 5-7 minutes for packaged egg and spinach noodles (to cook pasta, see p. 15).

Sauce:

3 tbsp./50 mL unsalted butter	_Melt butter in a skillet._
2 cups/500 mL whipping cream	_Add cream to skillet and stir until well blended._
1/2 lb./250 g walnuts, shelled and finely chopped (reserving 2-3 walnuts, shelled and halved, for garnish)	_Add walnuts to skillet and simmer for 4-5 minutes, allowing the flavour of the walnuts to mix with the cream, until sauce thickens slightly._
salt freshly ground black pepper	_Season with salt and pepper to taste._
	Add paglia e fieno to sauce in skillet. Toss and heat.
3/4 cup/175 mL Parmesan cheese, freshly grated	_Gradually add Parmesan cheese to paglia e fieno. Toss and heat until cheese has melted._
2 tsp./10 mL fresh parsley, finely chopped 3 walnuts, shelled and halved (reserved above)	_Put paglia e fieno on a warm serving platter or warm plates. Sprinkle with chopped fresh parsley. Garnish with halved walnuts and serve._

Paglia e Fieno con Quaglie

Straw and Hay with Roasted Quail

Serves 4-6

Cook 1/2 lb./250 g egg and 1/2 lb./250 g spinach noodles al dente: 3-5 minutes for fresh egg and spinach noodles; 5-7 minutes for packaged egg and spinach noodles (to cook pasta, see p. 15).

Sauce:

	Pre-heat oven to 400°F/200°C.
6 quail 12 slices of bacon 1 tsp./5 mL olive oil	_Wrap 2 slices of bacon around each quail. Sauté quail in olive oil in a skillet, turning frequently, until lightly browned._
	Put quail in a casserole dish. Put casserole dish in oven at 400°F/200°C and cook for 10 minutes.
a splash of dry white wine	_After 10 minutes cooking time, add a splash of white wine to casserole dish in oven and continue to cook for 5 minutes. When quail have finished cooking, remove casserole dish from oven. Allow quail to cool. When quail are cool,_

	remove bacon from quail and finely chop. Debone quail, reserving the meat, and set aside.
1/4 cup/50 mL dry Porcini mushrooms 2 cups/500 mL warm water	*Soak mushrooms in warm water in a bowl for 1 hour. Drain mushrooms and reserve liquid. Finely chop mushrooms. Strain liquid through a sieve lined with a linen or muslin cloth.*
1 cup/250 mL dry red wine	*Sauté mushrooms in red wine in a skillet for approximately 1 minute.*
mushroom liquid (reserved above)	*Add mushroom liquid to skillet and reduce by simmering for 2-3 minutes.*
	Add quail and bacon to skillet and cook until sauce thickens slightly.
salt freshly ground black pepper	*Season with salt and pepper to taste.*
	Add paglia e fieno to sauce in skillet. Toss and heat.
2-3 quail eggs, halved	*Put paglia e fieno on a warm serving platter or warm plates. Garnish with halved quail eggs and serve.*

Paglia e Fieno Alfredo

Serves 4-6

Straw and Hay in a Cream Sauce

Cook 1/2 lb./250 g egg and 1/2 lb./250 g spinach noodles al dente: 3-5 minutes for fresh egg and spinach noodles; 5-7 minutes for packaged egg and spinach noodles (to cook pasta, see p. 15).

Sauce:

1/2 cup/125 mL unsalted butter	*Melt butter in a skillet.*
1 1/2 cups/375 mL whipping cream	*Add cream to skillet and stir until well blended. Simmer for 3-4 minutes until sauce thickens slightly.*
salt freshly ground black pepper 1/8 tsp./pinch of ground nutmeg (optional)	*Season with salt, pepper and nutmeg.*
	Add paglia e fieno to sauce in skillet. Toss and heat.
3/4 cup/175 mL Parmesan cheese, freshly grated	*Add Parmesan cheese to paglia e fieno. Toss and heat until cheese has melted. (If sauce is too thick, add more cream.)*

(cont'd over)

4-6 tsp./20-30 mL Parmesan cheese, freshly grated	Put paglia e fieno on a warm serving platter or warm plates. Sprinkle with Parmesan cheese and chopped fresh parsley and serve.
4-6 tsp./20-30 mL fresh parsley, finely chopped	

P aglia e Fieno con Filettini di Vitello 4-6

Straw and Hay with a Julienne of Veal

Cook 1/2 lb./250 g egg and 1/2 lb./250 g spinach noodles al dente: 3-5 minutes for fresh egg and spinach noodles; 5-7 minutes for packaged egg and spinach noodles (to cook pasta, see p. 15).

Sauce:

3/4 lb./350 g loin of veal, julienned	Season veal with salt and pepper. Sauté veal in butter and vegetable oil in a skillet for 2-3 minutes until lightly browned. Drain oil from skillet.
salt	
white pepper	
1 tbsp./15 mL unsalted butter	
3 tbsp./50 mL vegetable oil	
2 tbsp./25 mL dry red wine	Add red and white wine to skillet and reduce by simmering for 1-2 minutes.
2 tbsp./25 mL dry white wine	
1 cup/250 mL beef consommé (see p. 20)	Add beef consommé and butter to skillet and simmer for 3-4 minutes until sauce thickens slightly.
2 tbsp./25 mL unsalted butter	
salt	Season with salt and pepper to taste.
white pepper	
	Add paglia e fieno to sauce in skillet. Toss and heat.
1/4 cup/50 mL Parmesan cheese, freshly grated	Add Parmesan cheese to paglia e fieno. Toss and heat.
1 tbsp./15 mL Parmesan cheese, freshly grated	Put paglia e fieno on a warm serving platter or warm plates. Sprinkle with Parmesan cheese and chopped fresh parsley and serve.
1 tbsp./15 mL fresh parsley, finely chopped	

Pappardelle

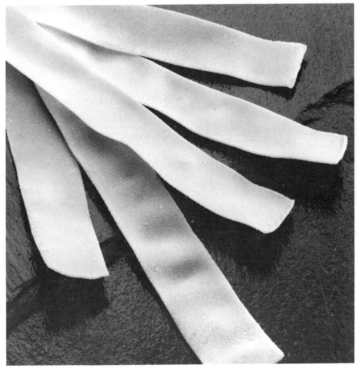

Pappardelle—thin, flat, broad pasta, cut by hand or by machine 1/2 to 3/4 inches/1–2 cm thick.

Pappardelle con Pollo Cacciatora

Serves 4-6

Pappardelle with Chicken, Onions and Olives

Cook 1 lb./500 g pappardelle al dente: 3-5 minutes for fresh pappardelle; 5-7 minutes for packaged pappardelle (to cook pasta, see p. 15).

Sauce:

6 firm, ripe tomatoes, eyes removed and scored "x" on top	*Blanch tomatoes in a pot of boiling water for 20 seconds, then plunge in cold water to stop the cooking. Peel, seed and chop tomatoes. Set aside.*
1/2 frying chicken or 1 double breast of chicken, deboned, with the skin and fat removed and reserved; the meat julienned 1 tbsp./15 mL olive oil salt freshly ground black pepper flour (to dust)	*Fry chicken skin and fat in olive oil in a skillet for 1-2 minutes. Remove skin and pieces of fat from skillet, reserving the oil and fat that has melted. Season chicken with salt and pepper. Lightly dust with flour. Sauté chicken in oil and fat in skillet until lightly browned.*
1/2 of 1 white onion, julienned	*Add onion to skillet and sauté for 1 minute until soft and transparent.*
1 clove garlic, crushed 12 Calamata black olives, pitted and sliced 12 stuffed Manzanilla green olives, sliced	*Add garlic and black and green olives to skillet and sauté for approximately 1 minute. Drain oil from skillet.*
2 tbsp./25 mL dry red wine 2 tbsp./25 mL dry white wine	*Add red and white wine to skillet and reduce by simmering for 1-2 minutes.*
1/8 tsp./pinch of hot red chili pepper 1 tbsp./15 mL unsalted butter	*Add tomatoes, chili pepper and butter to skillet and simmer for 2-3 minutes.*
salt freshly ground black pepper	*Season with salt and pepper to taste.*
	Add pappardelle to sauce in skillet. Toss and heat.
2 tbsp./25 mL fresh parsley, finely chopped 4-6 Calamata black olives, pitted and sliced	*Put pappardelle on a warm serving platter or warm plates. Sprinkle with chopped fresh parsley. Garnish with sliced Calamata black olives and serve.*

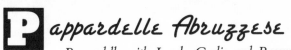appardelle Abruzzese

Pappardelle with Lamb, Garlic and Rosemary

Cook 1 lb./500 g pappardelle al dente: 3-5 minutes for fresh pappardelle; 5-7 minutes for packaged pappardelle (to cook pasta, see p. 15).

Sauce:

1 1/2 lbs./700 g loin of lamb, with the fat removed, then cubed salt freshly ground black pepper 1 tsp./5 mL fresh rosemary, crushed flour (to dust) 3 tbsp./50 mL olive oil	*Season lamb with salt and pepper. Sprinkle with rosemary. Lightly dust with flour. Sauté lamb in olive oil in a skillet for 10 minutes, turning frequently, until browned.*
1 1/2 tbsp./20 mL tomato paste	*Add tomato paste to skillet and stir until well blended.*
1/4 cup/50 mL dry full-bodied red wine	*Add red wine to skillet and reduce by simmering for 1-2 minutes.*
2 firm, ripe tomatoes, chopped 1 1/2 cups/375 mL beef consommé (see p. 20) 2 tbsp./25 mL unsalted butter	*Add tomatoes, beef consommé and butter to skillet and simmer for 4-5 minutes until sauce thickens slightly.*
salt freshly ground black pepper 1/2 tsp./2 mL garlic, crushed	*Season with salt, pepper and garlic.*
	Add pappardelle to sauce in skillet. Toss and heat.
4-6 tbsp./60-90 mL Parmesan cheese, freshly grated 4-6 sprigs of fresh rosemary	*Put pappardelle on a warm serving platter or warm plates. Sprinkle with Parmesan cheese. Garnish with sprigs of fresh rosemary and serve.*

Penne

Penne—"quill pens"—tubular pasta cut on an angle at the ends—comes smooth, or ridged as "penne rigate." When you see the word "rigate," it means the pasta has little ridges on it. The word for smooth in Italian is "liscio." Illustrated above is "penne lisce."

Illustration #7 (page 87): Paglia e Fieno con Filettini di Vitello/Straw and Hay with a Julienne of Veal photographed against Duchess Rose marble, courtesy of Quadra Stone Company Ltd.; serving platter courtesy of The Salt Box.

Illustration #8 (page 88): Penne Aglio e Olio/Penne Tossed with Pure Virgin Olive Oil and Garlic photographed against Rosso Levanto marble, courtesy of Quadra Stone Company Ltd.; plate courtesy of Umberto's Restaurants Ltd.

Penne Aglio e Olio

Serves 4-6

Penne Tossed with Pure Virgin Olive Oil and Garlic

Cook 1 lb./500 g penne al dente: 3-5 minutes for fresh penne; 7-9 minutes for packaged penne (to cook pasta, see p. 15). Drain and rinse. Put penne on a warm serving platter or warm plates.

3 tbsp./50 mL pure virgin olive oil	*Drizzle olive oil over penne.*
2 medium cloves garlic, finely chopped 1 tbsp./15 mL unsalted butter	*Add garlic and butter to penne and toss.*
salt freshly ground black pepper	*Season with salt and pepper to taste.*
4-6 tbsp./60-90 mL Parmesan cheese, freshly grated 2 tbsp./25 mL fresh parsley, finely chopped	*Sprinkle with Parmesan cheese and chopped fresh parsley and serve.*

Penne Casino

Serves 4-6

Penne with Hearts of Palm and Chervil

Cook 1 lb./500 g penne al dente: 3-5 minutes for fresh penne; 7-9 minutes for packaged penne (to cook pasta, see p. 15).

Sauce:

1 tbsp./15 mL shallot, finely chopped 1 tbsp./15 mL unsalted butter	*Sauté shallot in butter in a skillet for 1 minute until soft and transparent.*
1/4 cup/50 mL dry white wine	*Add white wine to skillet and reduce by simmering for 1-2 minutes.*
1 (14 oz./398 mL) can hearts of palm, drained, reserving 1/4 cup/ 50 mL hearts of palm liquid, with the hearts of palm quartered lengthwise, then halved	*Add hearts of palm liquid to skillet and simmer for approximately 2 minutes.*
2 tbsp./25 mL unsalted butter	*Add hearts of palm and butter to skillet and cook for approximately 2 minutes.*
salt freshly ground black pepper 6 tbsp./90 mL whole leaves of fresh chervil	*Season with salt, pepper and chervil.*
	Add penne to sauce in skillet. Toss and heat.
4-6 tbsp./60-90 mL Parmesan cheese, freshly grated 2 tbsp./25 mL tomato, concassé 4-6 sprigs of fresh chervil	*Put penne on a warm serving platter or warm plates. Sprinkle with Parmesan cheese. Garnish with tomato concassé and sprigs of fresh chervil and serve.*

Rigatoni

Rigatoni—1 1/2 inch/4 cm long round tubes, with ridges, approximately 1/2 inch/1 cm in diameter.

Rigatoni all' Indiana

Serves 4-6

Poppy Seed Rigatoni with Curry Sauce

Add poppy seeds to the flour and eggs when you're making the pasta (to make fresh pasta, see p. 10). Cook 1 lb./500 g rigatoni al dente: approximately 1 minute for fresh poppy seed rigatoni that you've just made (to cook pasta, see p. 15).

Sauce:

1 apple, with peel, quartered and cored 1 stalk celery, chopped 1 medium carrot, chopped 2 cups/500 mL dry white wine	*Simmer apple, celery and carrot in white wine in a saucepan until wine has reduced by one-half.*
	Put contents of saucepan in a blender or food processor and purée. Pour puréed apple-vegetable mixture into a skillet.
2 cups/500 mL whipping cream 3 tbsp./50 mL unsalted butter	*Add cream and butter to skillet and stir until well blended. Cook for 3-4 minutes until sauce thickens slightly.*
salt 2 tsp./10 mL curry powder	*Season with salt and curry powder.*
	Add poppy seed rigatoni to sauce in skillet. Toss and heat.
	Put rigatoni on a warm serving platter or warm plates and serve.

If you don't want to make poppy seed rigatoni, but want to use the sauce, cook egg rigatoni (5-7 minutes for fresh rigatoni; 10-15 minutes for packaged rigatoni) and add to sauce in skillet.

Rigatoni Bongusto

Serves 4-6

Herbed Rigatoni with Tomatoes, Olive Oil and Prosciutto

Add finely chopped fresh herbs to the flour and eggs when you're making the pasta (to make fresh pasta, see p. 10). Cook 1 lb./500 g rigatoni al dente: approximately 1 minute for fresh herbed rigatoni that you've just made (to cook pasta, see p. 15).

Sauce:

1/8 lb./50 g prosciutto, julienned 1 whole clove garlic 3 tbsp./50 mL olive oil	*Sauté prosciutto and garlic in olive oil in a skillet for 1 minute.*
1 (14 oz./398 mL) can Italian tomatoes, drained and quartered, reserving one-half of the tomato liquid	*Add tomatoes and one-half of the tomato liquid to skillet and simmer for 2 minutes. Remove garlic from skillet.*

(cont'd over)

91

12 leaves of fresh basil, julienned	*Add basil to skillet and stir until well blended.*
salt freshly ground black pepper	*Season with salt and pepper to taste.*
	Add herbed rigatoni to sauce in skillet. Toss and heat.
freshly ground black pepper 4-6 sprigs of fresh basil	*Put rigatoni on a warm serving platter or warm plates. Sprinkle with freshly ground black pepper. Garnish with sprigs of fresh basil and serve.*

If you don't want to make herbed rigatoni, but want to use the sauce, cook egg rigatoni (5-7 minutes for fresh rigatoni; 10-15 minutes for packaged rigatoni) and add to sauce in skillet.

 ## Rigatoni Romagnoli

Serves 4-6

Baked Rigatoni with Meat Sauce

Cook 1 lb./500 g rigatoni al dente: 5-7 minutes for fresh rigatoni; 10-15 minutes for packaged rigatoni (to cook pasta, see p. 15).

Sauce:

3 cups/750 mL meat sauce (see p. 18)	*Heat meat sauce in a skillet.*
salt freshly ground black pepper	*Season with salt and pepper to taste.*
	Add rigatoni to meat sauce in skillet. Toss and heat.
	Pre-heat oven to broil/grill.
1 tbsp./15 mL unsalted butter 2 tbsp./25 mL Béchamel sauce (see p. 18) 4-6 tbsp./60-90 mL Parmesan cheese, freshly grated	*Butter the bottom of a casserole dish. Put rigatoni and meat sauce mixture in casserole dish. Top with Béchamel sauce and Parmesan cheese.*
	Put casserole dish in oven and broil/grill until cheese is lightly browned. Remove casserole dish from oven.
2 tbsp./25 mL fresh parsley, finely chopped	*Sprinkle with chopped fresh parsley. Serve in casserole dish.*

Risotto

Risotto—Italian rice—comes in short grain and long grain. In this book, we have used short grain arborio rice (illustrated above). Note the kernel in the centre and the crude shape of the rice.

Risotto al Succo d'Uva Rossa

Risotto with Red Wine

Use short grained arborio rice.

2 cups/500 mL arborio rice	Wash rice in cold water and set aside.
2 shallots, finely chopped 2 tbsp./25 mL olive oil	Sauté shallots in olive oil in a skillet for 1 minute until soft and transparent.
1/2 cup/125 mL dry white wine	Put rice, shallots and white wine together in a pot and stir with a wooden spoon for 1-2 minutes. Begin to cook rice on medium heat.
1 1/2 cups/375 mL chicken consommé (see p. 21)	Using a ladle, add chicken consommé to rice every time rice becomes dry. Add chicken consommé a little at a time, always keeping rice moist and gently stirring after each addition. Add chicken consommé to rice for approximately 5 minutes.
2 cups/500 mL Barolo or Cabernet red wine	After 5 minutes, add red wine to rice every time rice becomes dry. Add red wine a little at a time. Always keep rice moist and gently stir after each addition. Cook for 10-13 minutes more. Total cooking time should be 15-18 minutes. Add red wine carefully at end of cooking time as rice absorbs more liquid then than at beginning. Rice is done when it is tender, but firm. Rice should always be creamy, not runny or sticky.
3 tbsp./50 mL unsalted butter 4 tbsp./60 mL Parmesan cheese, freshly grated	When rice is done, add butter and Parmesan cheese and stir.
salt freshly ground black pepper	Season with salt and pepper to taste.
	Put rice in a warm serving dish or on warm plates and serve immediately.

Risotto al Tartufo

Risotto with Black or White Truffles

Use short grained arborio rice.

2 cups/500 mL arborio rice	Wash rice in cold water and set aside.
2 shallots, finely chopped 2 tbsp./25 mL olive oil	Sauté shallots in olive oil in a skillet for 1 minute until soft and transparent.

1/2 cup/125 mL dry white wine	*Put rice, shallots and white wine together in a pot and stir with a wooden spoon for 1-2 minutes. Begin to cook rice on medium heat.*
1 (.45 oz./12.5 g) can black or white truffles, drained, reserving the liquid 1/2 cup/125 mL chicken consommé (see p. 21)	*Put truffles and chicken consommé in a blender or food processor and purée. Add truffle purée to rice and gently stir. Reserve truffle liquid and set aside.*
3 cups/750 mL chicken consommé (see p. 21)	*When truffle purée has been added to rice, using a ladle, add chicken consommé to rice every time rice becomes dry. Add chicken consommé a little at a time, always keeping rice moist and gently stirring after each addition. Add chicken consommé to rice for 12-15 minutes.*
truffle liquid (reserved above)	*After 12-15 minutes, add truffle liquid to rice every time rice becomes dry. Cook for approximately 3 minutes more. Total cooking time should be 15-18 minutes. Add truffle liquid carefully at end of cooking time as rice absorbs more liquid then than at beginning. Rice is done when it is tender, but firm. Rice should always be creamy, not runny or sticky.*
3 tbsp./50 mL unsalted butter 4 tbsp./60 mL Parmesan cheese, freshly grated	*When rice is done, add butter and Parmesan cheese and stir.*
salt freshly ground black pepper	*Season with salt and pepper to taste.*
	Put rice in a warm serving dish or on warm plates and serve immediately.

R isotto all' Aragosta

Risotto with Lobster Tails

Serves 4-6

Use short grained arborio rice.

2 cups/500 mL arborio rice	*Wash rice in cold water and set aside.*
2 shallots, finely chopped 2 tbsp./25 mL olive oil	*Sauté shallots in olive oil in a skillet for 1 minute until soft and transparent.*
1/2 cup/125 mL dry white wine	*Put rice, shallots and white wine together in a pot and stir with a wooden spoon for 1-2 minutes. Begin to cook rice on medium heat.*
4 cups/1 L fish consommé (see p. 20)	*Using a ladle, add fish stock to rice every time rice becomes dry. Add fish stock a little at a time, always keeping rice moist and gently*

(cont'd over)

	stirring after each addition. Cook rice for a total of 15-18 minutes.
2 medium fresh lobster tails, shells off, peeled and deveined, then cut in medallions 1/2 inch/1 cm thick 3 tbsp./50 mL fresh cilantro, finely chopped	*Approximately 4 minutes before rice has finished cooking, add medallions of lobster and cilantro to pot and gently stir. Add fish stock to rice throughout cooking time, but add carefully at end of cooking time as rice absorbs more liquid then than at beginning. Rice is done when it is tender, but firm. Rice should always be creamy, not runny or sticky.*
salt white pepper	*Season with salt and pepper to taste.*
	Put rice in a warm serving dish or on warm plates and serve immediately.

 isotto con Asparagi   *Serves 4-6*

Risotto with Asparagus

Use short grained arborio rice.

2 cups/500 mL arborio rice	*Wash rice in cold water and set aside.*
3/4 lb./350 g fresh asparagus	*Blanch asparagus in a saucepan of boiling water for 3-4 minutes. Drain asparagus and set aside. Keep warm. Reserve 8-12 asparagus tips for garnish.*
2 shallots, finely chopped 2 tbsp./25 mL olive oil	*Sauté shallots in olive oil in a skillet for 1 minute until soft and transparent.*
1/2 cup/125 mL dry white wine	*Put rice, shallots and white wine together in a pot and stir with a wooden spoon for 1-2 minutes. Begin to cook rice on medium heat.*
4 cups/1 L chicken consommé (see p. 21)	*Using a ladle, add chicken consommé to rice every time rice becomes dry. Add chicken consommé a little at a time, always keeping rice moist and gently stirring after each addition. Cook rice for a total of 15-18 minutes.*
	Approximately 2 minutes before rice has finished cooking, add asparagus and gently stir. Add chicken consommé to rice throughout cooking time, but add carefully at end of cooking time as rice absorbs more liquid then than at beginning. Rice is done when it is tender, but firm. Rice should always be creamy, not runny or sticky.
3 tbsp./50 mL unsalted butter 4 tbsp./60 mL Parmesan cheese, freshly grated	*When rice is done, add butter and Parmesan cheese and stir.*

salt white pepper	Season with salt and pepper to taste.
8-12 asparagus tips (reserved above)	Put rice in a warm serving dish or on warm plates. Garnish with asparagus tips and serve immediately.

Risotto con Funghi Affumicati

Serves 4-6

Risotto with Smoked Mushrooms

Use short grained arborio rice.

1/4 cup/50 mL dry smoked mushrooms—Porcini mushrooms 2 cups/500 mL warm water	Soak mushrooms in warm water in a bowl for 1 hour. Drain mushrooms and reserve liquid. Finely chop mushrooms. Strain liquid through a sieve lined with a linen or muslin cloth.
2 cups/500 mL arborio rice	Wash rice in cold water and set aside.
2 shallots, finely chopped 2 tbsp./25 mL olive oil	Sauté shallots in olive oil in a skillet for 1 minute until soft and transparent.
1/2 cup/125 mL dry white wine	Put rice, shallots and white wine together in a pot and stir with a wooden spoon for 1-2 minutes. Begin to cook rice on medium heat.
2 cups/500 mL chicken consommé (see p. 21)	Using a ladle, add chicken consommé to rice every time rice becomes dry. Add chicken consommé a little at a time, always keeping rice moist and gently stirring after each addition. Add chicken consommé to rice for 8-9 minutes.
mushroom liquid (reserved above)	After 8-9 minutes, add mushrooms to rice, and add mushroom liquid every time rice becomes dry. Add mushroom liquid a little at a time. Always keep rice moist and gently stir after each addition. Cook for 7-9 minutes more. Total cooking time should be 15-18 minutes. Add mushroom liquid carefully at end of cooking time as rice absorbs more liquid then than at beginning. Rice is done when it is tender, but firm. Rice should always be creamy, not runny or sticky.
3 tbsp./50 mL unsalted butter 4 tbsp./60 mL Parmesan cheese, freshly grated	When rice is done, add butter and Parmesan cheese and stir.
salt freshly ground black pepper	Season with salt and pepper to taste.
	Put rice in a warm serving dish or on warm plates and serve immediately.

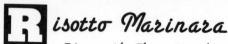

Risotto Marinara

Serves 4-6

Risotto with Clams, Mussels, Shrimp and Peas

Use short grained arborio rice.

2 cups/500 mL arborio rice	*Wash rice in cold water and set aside.*
16-24 fresh clams, washed and cleaned 16-24 fresh mussels, washed and cleaned 1/4 cup/50 mL cold water 1/4 cup/50 mL dry white wine 1 medium clove garlic, finely chopped	*Put clams and mussels in a large pot with water, white wine and garlic. Cover pot, bring to a boil and steam clams and mussels for 5-6 minutes until their shells open. Set clams and mussels, in shells, aside. Reserve liquid and set aside.*
2 shallots, finely chopped 2 tbsp./25 mL olive oil	*Sauté shallots in olive oil in a skillet for 1 minute until soft and transparent.*
1/2 cup/125 mL dry white wine	*Put rice, shallots and white wine together in a pot and stir with a wooden spoon for 1-2 minutes. Begin to cook rice on medium heat.*
3 cups/750 mL fish consommé (see p. 20)	*Using a ladle, add fish stock to rice every time rice becomes dry. Add fish stock a little at a time, always keeping rice moist and gently stirring after each addition. Add fish stock to rice for approximately 10 minutes.*
16-24 steamed clams, in the shell (reserved above) 16-24 steamed mussels, in the shell (reserved above) 1 cup/250 mL fresh shrimp, peeled and cleaned 1 cup/250 mL peas clam and mussel liquid (reserved above)	*After 10 minutes, add clams and mussels in the shell to pot, reserving 4-6 clams and 4-6 mussels in the shell for garnish. Add shrimp and peas to pot, and add clam and mussel liquid every time rice becomes dry. Add clam and mussel liquid a little at a time. Always keep rice moist and gently stir after each addition. Cook for 5-8 minutes more. Total cooking time should be 15-18 minutes. Add clam and mussel liquid carefully at end of cooking time as rice absorbs more liquid then than at beginning. Rice is done when it is tender, but firm. Rice should always be creamy, not runny or sticky.*
salt freshly ground black pepper	*Season with salt and pepper to taste.*
1 tbsp./15 mL fresh parsley, finely chopped 4-6 steamed clams, in the shell (reserved above) 4-6 steamed mussels, in the shell (reserved above)	*Put rice in a warm serving dish or on warm plates. Sprinkle with chopped fresh parsley. Garnish with clams and mussels in the shell and serve immediately.*

Rotini

Rotini—thick spiral shaped pasta—screw shaped—like fusilli, only broader.

Rotini con Uova di Salmone

Beet Rotini with Salmon Roe

Serves 4-6

Add puréed beets to the flour and eggs when you're making the pasta (to make fresh coloured pasta, see p. 10). Cook 1 lb./500 g rotini al dente: 1 minute for fresh beet rotini that you've just made (to cook pasta, see p. 15).

Sauce:

1 cup/250 mL unsalted butter 2 tbsp./25 mL shallots, finely chopped 2 tbsp./25 mL fresh parsley, finely chopped 2 tbsp./25 mL fresh chervil, finely chopped 1/4 cup/50 mL dry white wine salt freshly ground black pepper juice of 1/2 lemon	*Make a herb butter by putting butter, shallots, parsley, chervil, white wine, salt, pepper and lemon juice in a blender or food processor and mixing together.*
1/4 cup/50 mL dry white wine	*Heat white wine in a skillet, then add herb butter. Allow butter to melt and, using a whisk, stir until well blended. Simmer for approximately 2 minutes.* *Add beet rotini to sauce in skillet. Toss and heat.*
4-6/ tbsp./60-90 mL red salmon caviar	*Add caviar to rotini and gently toss. (Don't be afraid to break the caviar.)*
2 tbsp./25 mL vodka	*Add vodka to rotini and toss one more time.*
1 tbsp./15 mL fresh parsley, finely chopped freshly ground black pepper 1 lemon, cut in rounds 4-6 tsp./20-30 mL red salmon caviar	*Put rotini on a warm serving platter or warm plates. Sprinkle with chopped fresh parsley and freshly ground black pepper. Garnish with lemon rounds with caviar in the centre of each round and serve.*

If you don't want to make beet rotini, but want to use the sauce, cook egg rotini (3-5 minutes for fresh rotini; 5-7 minutes for packaged rotini) and add to sauce in skillet.

Rotini Novelli

Rotini with a Julienne of Sole and Avocado

Serves 4-6

Cook 1 lb./500 g rotini al dente: 3-5 minutes for fresh rotini; 5-7 minutes for packaged rotini (to cook pasta, see p. 15).

Sauce:

2 medium firm, ripe avocados, peeled, quartered and sliced juice of 1/2 lemon	*Put avocado in a bowl and sprinkle with lemon juice. Set aside.*

1 lb./500 g fillet of fresh, firm sole, washed and dried, then julienned salt white pepper flour (to dust) 1/2 cup/125 mL vegetable oil 1 tbsp./15 mL unsalted butter	*Season sole with salt and pepper. Lightly dust with flour. Heat oil in a skillet and add butter. When butter foams, add sole and quickly sauté until golden brown. Remove sole from skillet and pat dry with a cloth. Discard oil and butter from skillet.*
2 shallots, finely chopped 1 tbsp./15 mL unsalted butter	*Sauté shallots in butter in same skillet for 1 minute until soft and transparent.*
1/2 cup/125 mL dry white wine	*Add white wine to skillet and reduce by simmering for 2-3 minutes.*
1/2 cup/125 mL fish stock (see p. 20)	*Add fish stock to skillet and cook for approximately 2 minutes.*
1 cup/250 mL whipping cream	*Add cream to skillet and stir until well blended. Reduce by simmering for 4-5 minutes until sauce thickens slightly.*
2 tbsp./25 mL unsalted butter	*Add butter to sauce and blend in. Cook until sauce is smooth and velvety.*
	Add avocados to skillet and cook for approximately 2 minutes.
1 firm, ripe tomato, eye removed and scored "x" on top	*Blanch tomato in a pot of boiling water for 20 seconds, then plunge in cold water to stop the cooking. Peel, seed and julienne tomato.*
	Return sole to skillet and add tomato. Cook for approximately 1 minute. (Don't worry if the sole crumbles.)
salt white pepper 1/2 tsp./2 mL fresh thyme, finely chopped	*Season with salt, pepper and thyme.*
	Add rotini to sauce in skillet. Gently toss and heat.
4-6 sprigs of fresh thyme	*Put rotini on a warm serving platter or warm plates. Garnish with sprigs of fresh thyme and serve.*

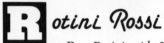

Rotini Rossi

Beet Rotini with Herb Butter

Add puréed beets to the flour and eggs when you're making the pasta (to make fresh coloured pasta, see p. 10). Cook 1 lb./500 g rotini al dente: approximately 1 minute for fresh beet rotini that you've just made (to cook pasta, see p. 15).

Sauce:

2 medium red beets, tip and leaves chopped off cold water (to cover)	*Boil beets in water in a saucepan for 30 minutes until tender, then run them under cold water. Peel, slice and julienne beets. Set aside.*
1 cup/250 mL unsalted butter 2 tbsp./25 mL shallots, finely chopped 1 tsp./5 mL fresh basil, finely chopped 1 tsp./5 mL fresh sage, finely chopped 1 tsp./5 mL fresh thyme, finely chopped salt freshly ground black pepper juice of 1/2 lemon	*Make a herb butter by putting butter, shallots, basil, sage, thyme, salt, pepper and lemon juice in a blender or food processor and mixing together.*
1/4 cup/50 mL dry white wine 1/2 cup/125 mL chicken consommé (see p. 21)	*Put beets in a skillet. Add white wine and chicken consommé to skillet and reduce by simmering for 3-4 minutes.*
	Add herb butter to skillet and allow butter to melt. Using a whisk, stir until well blended. Simmer for approximately 2 minutes.
salt freshly ground black pepper	*Season with salt and pepper to taste.*
	Add beet rotini to sauce in skillet. Toss and heat.
4-6 tsp./20-30 mL whole leaves of fresh chervil	*Put rotini on a warm serving platter or warm plates. Garnish with whole leaves of fresh chervil and serve.*

If you don't want to make beet rotini, but want to use the sauce, cook egg rotini (3-5 minutes for fresh rotini; 5-7 minutes for packaged rotini) and add to sauce in skillet.

Rotini Shakespeare

Rotini with a Julienne of Pork and Prunes

Cook 1 lb./500 g rotini al dente: 3-5 minutes for fresh rotini; 5-7 minutes for packaged rotini (to cook pasta, see p. 15).

Sauce:

1/2 lb./250 g loin of pork, julienned salt freshly ground black pepper 1/4 tsp./1 mL fresh ginger, finely chopped 1/2 tsp./2 mL fresh oregano, finely chopped flour (to dust) 1/2 cup/125 mL vegetable oil	*Season pork with salt and pepper. Sprinkle with ginger and oregano. Lightly dust with flour. Sauté pork in vegetable oil in a skillet until lightly browned. Remove pork from skillet and set aside. Drain oil from skillet.*
1/2 of 1 purple onion, julienned 1 tbsp./15 mL unsalted butter	*Sauté onion in butter in same skillet for 1 minute until soft and transparent.*
1/2 cup/125 mL semi-sweet white wine	*Deglaze skillet with white wine.*
1 cup/250 mL fresh or dried prunes, pitted and julienned	*Add prunes to skillet and cook for approximately 2 minutes.*
1/2 cup/125 mL chicken consommé (see p. 21) 2 tbsp./25 mL unsalted butter	*Add chicken consommé and butter to skillet and simmer for 2-3 minutes.*
	Return pork to skillet and cook for approximately 2 minutes.
salt freshly ground black pepper	*Season with salt and pepper to taste.*
	Add rotini to sauce in skillet. Toss and heat.
1/4 cup/50 mL Fontina cheese, freshly grated 4-6 sprigs of fresh oregano	*Put rotini on a warm serving platter or warm plates. Sprinkle with Fontina cheese. Garnish with sprigs of fresh oregano and serve.*

Sedanini

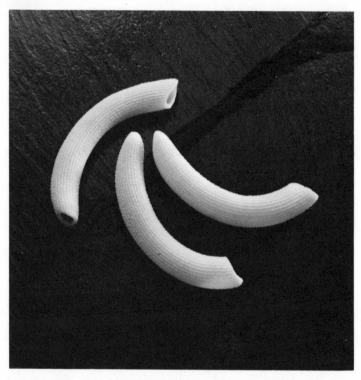

Sedanini — "little celeries" — long, thin, tubular pasta, with ridges, like celery with its threads, only densely threaded.

Illustration #9 (page 105): Risotto Marinara/Risotto with Clams, Mussels, Shrimp and Peas photographed against Violet Moresque marble, courtesy of Quadra Stone Company Ltd.; plate courtesy of Umberto's Restaurants Ltd.

Illustration #10 (page 106): Sedanini Siciliana/Sedanini with Tomatoes, Green and Black Olives, Anchovies and Capers photographed against Rosa del Monte marble, courtesy of Quadra Stone Company Ltd.; serving dish courtesy of The Salt Box.

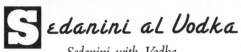# **S**edanini al Vodka

Sedanini with Vodka

Cook 1 lb./500 g sedanini al dente: 3-5 minutes for fresh sedanini; 10-15 minutes for packaged sedanini (to cook pasta, see p. 15).

Sauce:

1/4 lb./125 g bacon, chopped 1/2 of 1 white onion, chopped 2 stalks celery, chopped 1 medium carrot, chopped 2 firm, ripe tomatoes, eyes removed	*Fry bacon in a skillet until just done — not crisp. Drain bacon on paper towels. Put bacon and vegetables in a blender or food processor and purée.*
2 tbsp./25 mL olive oil	*Cook bacon and vegetable purée in olive oil in a skillet for approximately 2 minutes.*
a splash of dry white wine 2 tbsp./25 mL vodka	*Add white wine and vodka to skillet and simmer for 1 minute until sauce thickens slightly.*
salt white pepper	*Season with salt and pepper to taste.*
	Add sedanini to sauce in skillet. Toss and heat.
1/4 cup/50 mL Parmesan cheese, freshly grated 1 tbsp./15 mL fresh parsley, finely chopped	*Put sedanini on a warm serving platter or warm plates. Sprinkle with Parmesan cheese and chopped fresh parsley and serve.*

Sedanini alla Svizzera

Sedanini with Assorted Mushrooms and Smoked Gruyère Cheese

Cook 1 lb./500 g sedanini al dente: 3-5 minutes for fresh sedanini; 10-15 minutes for packaged sedanini (to cook pasta, see p. 15).

Sauce:

2 shallots, finely chopped 2 tbsp./25 mL unsalted butter	*Sauté shallots in butter in a skillet for 1 minute until soft and transparent.*
1/4 lb./125 g fresh Chanterelle mushrooms, cleaned and sliced 1/4 lb./125 g fresh Cèpes or Boletus mushrooms, cleaned and sliced 1/4 lb./125 g fresh Oyster mushrooms, cleaned and sliced — or 1/4 lb./125 g fresh champignon mushrooms, cleaned and sliced 1 tbsp./15 mL unsalted butter	*Add mushrooms and butter to skillet and sauté for approximately 4 minutes.*

(cont'd over)

1/4 cup/50 mL dry white wine	*Add white wine to skillet and reduce by simmering for 1-2 minutes.*
1/2 cup/125 mL chicken consommé (see p. 21)	*Add chicken consommé to skillet and simmer for 2-3 minutes.*
1/2 cup/125 mL whipping cream	*Add cream to skillet and stir until well blended. Reduce by simmering for 2-3 minutes until sauce thickens slightly.*
salt white pepper 1/2 tsp./2 mL fresh thyme, finely chopped	*Season with salt, pepper and thyme.*
	Add sedanini to sauce in skillet. Toss and heat.
	Pre-heat oven to broil/grill.
1 cup/250 mL smoked Gruyère cheese, freshly grated 1/4 lb./125 g fresh wild Japanese shiitake mushrooms 4-6 sprigs of fresh thyme	*Put sedanini in a large casserole dish. Sprinkle with smoked Gruyère cheese. Put casserole dish in oven and broil/grill until cheese is lightly browned. Remove casserole dish from oven and garnish with whole fresh wild Japanese shiitake mushrooms and sprigs of fresh thyme. Serve in casserole dish.*

edanini di Pollo Vellutati

Serves 4-6

Sedanini with Chicken and Juniper Berries

Cook 1 lb./500 g sedanini al dente: 3-5 minutes for fresh sedanini; 10-15 minutes for packaged sedanini (to cook pasta, see p. 15).

Sauce:

2 tbsp./25 mL juniper berries, chopped 1/4 cup/50 mL dry white wine 1/3 cup/75 mL chicken consommé (see p. 21)	*Simmer juniper berries in white wine and chicken consommé in a skillet for 10 minutes. Set aside.*
3/4 lb./350 g breast of chicken, julienned salt white pepper 3 tbsp./50 mL olive oil	*Season chicken with salt and pepper. Sauté chicken in olive oil in a skillet until lightly browned.*
2 tbsp./25 mL gin	*Add gin to skillet and simmer until gin has evaporated. Remove chicken from skillet and set aside.*

2 medium leeks, washed and cleaned, with the root and leaves discarded and cut in rings 1/4 inch/.5 cm thick — use just the white part 2 tbsp./25 mL unsalted butter	*Sauté leeks in butter in same skillet for 3-4 minutes, stirring constantly.*
2 tbsp./25 mL dry white wine	*Add white wine to skillet and simmer until wine has evaporated.*
	Strain juniper berry liquid into skillet.
1 cup/250 mL whipping cream	*Add cream to skillet and stir until well blended. Reduce by simmering for 4-5 minutes until sauce thickens slightly.*
	Return chicken to skillet and cook for 1-2 minutes.
4 tbsp./60 mL unsalted butter	*Add butter to sauce and blend in. Cook until sauce is smooth and velvety.*
salt white pepper	*Season with salt and pepper to taste.*
	Add sedanini to sauce in skillet. Toss and heat.
4-6 tbsp./60-90 mL Parmesan cheese, freshly grated	*Put sedanini on a warm serving platter or warm plates. Sprinkle with Parmesan cheese and serve.*

Sedanini Carbonara

Serves 4-6

Sedanini with Ham, Eggs and Cream

Cook 1 lb./500 g sedanini al dente: 3-5 minutes for fresh sedanini; 10-15 minutes for packaged sedanini (to cook pasta, see p. 15).

Sauce:

1/4 lb./125 g prosciutto, julienned 1 tbsp./15 mL unsalted butter	*Sauté prosciutto in butter in a skillet for 1-2 minutes until it is soft.*
2 cups/500 mL whipping cream	*Add cream to skillet and slowly bring to a boil.*
freshly ground black pepper	*Season with pepper only. (The prosciutto should give you enough salt.)*
	Add sedanini to sauce in skillet. Toss and heat.
1/2 cup/125 mL Parmesan cheese, freshly grated	*Gradually add Parmesan cheese to sedanini. Toss and heat until cheese has melted.*
2 egg yolks	*Remove skillet from heat. Add egg yolks to sedanini and quickly toss.*
1/2 cup/125 mL Parmesan cheese, freshly grated 2 tsp./10 mL fresh parsley, finely chopped	*Put sedanini on a warm serving platter or warm plates. Sprinkle with Parmesan cheese and chopped fresh parsley and serve.*

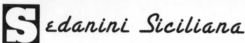

Sedanini Siciliana

Sedanini with Tomatoes, Green and Black Olives, Anchovies and Capers

Cook 1 lb./500 g sedanini al dente: 3-5 minutes for fresh sedanini; 10-15 minutes for packaged sedanini (to cook pasta, see p. 15).

Sauce:

3 firm, ripe tomatoes, eyes removed and scored "x" on top	*Blanch tomatoes in a pot of boiling water for 20 seconds, then plunge in cold water to stop the cooking. Peel, seed and chop tomatoes. Set aside.*
1/2 of 1 white onion, diced 3 tbsp./50 mL olive oil	*Sauté onion in olive oil in a skillet for 1 minute until soft and transparent.*
2 cloves garlic, crushed 3 fillets of anchovy, washed and mashed	*Add garlic and anchovies to skillet and toss for 1 minute.*
	Add tomatoes to skillet and simmer for 4 minutes.
10 black Calamata olives, pitted and chopped 10 green Calamata olives, pitted and chopped 3 tbsp./50 mL capers, drained	*Add black and green olives and capers to skillet and stir until well blended.*
1/4 cup/50 mL chicken consommé (see p. 21)	*Add chicken consommé to skillet and simmer for 4 minutes.*
salt freshly ground black pepper	*Season with salt and pepper to taste. (Be careful with the salt as anchovies and olives are salty to begin with.)*
	Add sedanini to sauce in skillet. Toss and heat.
4-6 tbsp./60-90 mL Parmesan cheese, freshly grated 1 tbsp./15 mL capers, drained 2 fillets of anchovy, washed and julienned	*Put sedanini on a warm serving platter or warm plates. Sprinkle with Parmesan cheese. Garnish with capers and julienned anchovies and serve.*

Spaghetti

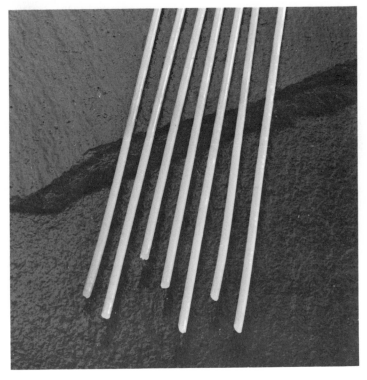

Spaghetti—round, thin, long pasta—probably the best-known pasta in the world.

Spaghetti Amatriciana

Spaghetti with Tomatoes, Onion, Bacon and Cheese

Serves 4-6

Cook 1 lb./500 g spaghetti al dente: 3-5 minutes for fresh spaghetti; 5-7 minutes for packaged spaghetti (to cook pasta, see p. 15).

Sauce:

1 medium white onion, finely chopped 1 tsp./5 mL unsalted butter 1 tsp./5 mL olive oil	*Sauté onion in butter and olive oil in a skillet for 1 minute until soft and transparent.*
1/4 lb./125 g smoked bacon or prosciutto, finely diced	*Add smoked bacon or prosciutto to skillet and sauté for 2-3 minutes.*
3 firm, ripe tomatoes, finely chopped 2 cloves garlic, finely chopped 1 tbsp./15 mL dry white wine	*Add tomatoes, garlic and white wine to skillet and simmer for 3-4 minutes.*
freshly ground black pepper	*Season with pepper only. (The smoked bacon or prosciutto should give you enough salt.)*
	Add spaghetti to sauce in skillet. Toss and heat.
1/4 cup/50 mL Pecorino Romano cheese, freshly grated	*Put spaghetti on a warm serving platter or warm plates. Sprinkle with Pecorino Romano cheese and serve.*

Spaghetti Bolognese

Spaghetti with Meat Sauce

Serves 4-6

Cook 1 lb./500 g spaghetti al dente: 3-5 minutes for fresh spaghetti; 5-7 minutes for packaged spaghetti (to cook pasta, see p. 15).

Sauce:

3 cups/750 mL meat sauce (see p. 18)	*Heat meat sauce in a skillet.*
salt freshly ground black pepper	*Season with salt and pepper to taste.*
	Add spaghetti to meat sauce in skillet. Toss and heat.
1/4 cup/50 mL Parmesan cheese, freshly grated	*Put spaghetti on a warm serving platter or warm plates. Sprinkle with Parmesan cheese and serve.*

# Spaghetti Marinara

Spaghetti with Clams and Tomatoes

Cook 1 lb./500 g spaghetti al dente: 3-5 minutes for fresh spaghetti; 5-7 minutes for packaged spaghetti (to cook pasta, see p. 15).

Sauce:

6 lbs./3 kg fresh clams, washed and cleaned, or 2 (5 oz./142 g) cans clams, reserving the liquid 2 cups/500 mL cold water 1/4 cup/50 mL dry white wine 1 small white onion, finely diced 1 bay leaf	*For fresh clams, put clams in a pot and add water, white wine, onion and bay leaf. Cover pot, bring to a boil and steam clams for 5-6 minutes until their shells open. Drain pot, reserving 1/2 cup/125 mL of liquid. Remove clams from shells and set aside.*
2 shallots, finely chopped 2 cloves garlic, finely chopped 3 tbsp./50 mL unsalted butter	*Sauté shallots and garlic in butter in a skillet for 1-2 minutes until shallots are soft and transparent.*
3/4 cup/175 mL dry white wine or dry white vermouth	*Add white wine or vermouth to skillet and reduce by simmering for 1-2 minutes.*
2 tbsp./25 mL fresh parsley, finely chopped	*Add clams, clam liquid and parsley to skillet and stir until well blended. Simmer for 2-3 minutes.*
4 firm, ripe tomatoes, eyes removed and scored "x" on top	*Blanch tomatoes in a pot of boiling water for 20 seconds, then plunge in cold water to stop the cooking. Peel, seed and chop tomatoes.*
3/4 cup/175 mL tomato sauce (see p. 19)	*Add tomatoes and tomato sauce to skillet and stir until well blended. Simmer for approximately 10 minutes.*
salt freshly ground black pepper	*Season with salt and pepper to taste. (Be careful with the salt as clams may be salty to begin with.)*
	Add spaghetti to sauce in skillet. Toss and heat.
1 tbsp./15 mL fresh parsley, finely chopped	*Put spaghetti on a warm serving platter or warm plates. Sprinkle with chopped fresh parsley and serve. Cheese not recommended.*

Tortellini

Tortellini—"little twists"—rumoured to have been modelled after Venus' navel—come in egg noodle tortellini and spinach tortellini. The egg noodle tortellini is usually stuffed with chicken or veal; the spinach tortellini is usually stuffed with cheese. Illustrated above is egg noodle tortellini.

Tortellini alla Panna

Tortellini with Cream Sauce

Cook 1 lb./500 g egg or spinach tortellini al dente: 7-10 minutes for fresh tortellini; 10-15 minutes for packaged tortellini (to cook pasta, see p. 15). Drain and rinse. Put tortellini in a bowl. Add 1 tbsp./15 mL olive oil to tortellini. The oil prevents the pasta sticking. Set aside.

Sauce:

2 cups/500 mL whipping cream	*Put cream in a skillet and slowly bring to a boil.*
salt freshly ground black pepper	*Season with salt and pepper to taste.*
	Add tortellini to cream in skillet. Toss and heat.
2 cups/500 mL Parmesan cheese, freshly grated	*Gradually add Parmesan cheese to tortellini. Toss and heat until cheese has melted and sauce has thickened.*
1/2 cup/125 mL Parmesan cheese, freshly grated 1 tbsp./15 mL fresh parsley, finely chopped	*Put tortellini on a warm serving platter or warm plates. Sprinkle with Parmesan cheese and chopped fresh parsley and serve.*

Tortellini in Brodo

Tortellini in Chicken Consommé

Cook 24-36 egg tortellini al dente: 7-10 minutes for fresh tortellini; 10-15 minutes for packaged tortellini (to cook pasta, see p. 15). Drain and rinse. Put tortellini in a bowl. Add 1 tbsp./15 mL olive oil to tortellini. The oil prevents the pasta sticking. Set aside.

4 cups/1 L chicken consommé (see p. 21)	*Put chicken consommé in a pot and bring to a boil.*
	Reduce heat, add tortellini to pot and simmer for approximately 5 minutes.
	Ladle soup into a warm soup tureen or into warm bowls—6 tortellini per bowl.
4-6 tbps./60-90 mL Parmesan cheese, freshly grated 4-6 tsp./20-30 mL fresh parsley, finely chopped	*Sprinkle with Parmesan cheese and chopped fresh parsley and serve.*

Tortellini Piccanti

Tortellini with Garlic, Sage and Pimento

Cook 1 lb./500 g egg tortellini al dente: 7-10 minutes for fresh tortellini; 10-15 minutes for packaged tortellini (to cook pasta, see p. 15). Drain and rinse. Put tortellini in a bowl. Add 1 tbsp./15 mL olive oil to tortellini. The oil prevents the pasta sticking. Set aside.

Sauce:

3 medium cloves garlic, finely chopped 2 tbsp./25 mL unsalted butter 2 tbsp./25 mL olive oil	*Sauté garlic in butter and olive oil in a skillet for approximately 1 minute.*
7 leaves of fresh sage, finely chopped 1 (14 oz./398 mL) can of pimento, chopped 1/4 cup/50 mL chicken consommé (see p. 21)	*Add sage, pimento and chicken consommé to skillet and simmer for 3-4 minutes.*
2 tbsp./25 mL unsalted butter	*Add butter to skillet and stir until well blended. Simmer for approximately 2 minutes.*
salt freshly ground black pepper	*Season with salt and pepper to taste.*
	Add tortellini to sauce in skillet. Toss and heat.
2 tbsp./25 mL Parmesan cheese, freshly grated	*Add Parmesan cheese to tortellini. Toss and heat.*
4-6 tsp./20-30 mL Parmesan cheese, freshly grated 4-6 sprigs of fresh sage	*Put tortellini on a warm serving platter or warm plates. Sprinkle with Parmesan cheese. Garnish with sprigs of fresh sage and serve.*

Ziti

Ziti—"bridegrooms"—long tubular pasta, stick like, which are broken into pieces to be cooked.

Ziti con Granchio Mandorlato

Serves 4-6

Ziti with Crab, Horseradish, Butter Lettuce and Toasted Almonds

Cook 1 lb./500 g ziti al dente: 3-5 minutes for fresh ziti; 5-7 minutes for packaged ziti (to cook pasta, see p. 15).

Sauce:

1/2 cup/125 mL dry white wine 2 cups/500 mL fish consommé (see p. 20)	*Mix white wine and fish stock together in a skillet and bring to a boil.*
1 lb./500 g fresh crabmeat 1 medium head butter lettuce, washed and cored, then julienned	*Add crabmeat and butter lettuce to skillet and cook for approximately 1 minute.*
3 tbsp./50 mL unsalted butter 2 tbsp./25 mL horseradish 1/4 cup/50 mL sliced almonds, toasted	*Add butter, horseradish and toasted almonds to skillet and stir until well blended.*
salt white pepper	*Season with salt and pepper to taste.*
	Add ziti to sauce in skillet. Toss and heat.
	Put ziti on a warm serving platter or warm plates and serve.

Ziti dell' Ortolano

Serves 4-6

Ziti with Mixed Vegetables and Pure Virgin Olive Oil

Cook 1 lb./500 g ziti al dente: 3-5 minutes for fresh ziti; 5-7 minutes for packaged ziti (to cook pasta, see p. 15).

1/2 of 1 white onion, sliced 3 tbsp./50 mL olive oil	*Sauté onion in olive oil in a skillet until lightly browned.*
2 cloves garlic, finely chopped	*Add garlic to skillet and quickly toss for 1 minute.*
1 medium zucchini, washed, dried and cubed 1 eggplant, washed, dried and cubed 1 red bell pepper, washed, halved and seeded 1 green bell pepper, washed, halved and seeded 1 firm, ripe tomato, washed, chopped and seeded	*Add vegetables to skillet and cook al dente. This should take no longer than 4-5 minutes.*

salt freshly ground black pepper 6 leaves of fresh basil, julienned 4 leaves of fresh oregano, finely chopped — or 1 tsp./5 mL dry oregano	*Season with salt, pepper, basil and oregano.*
	Add ziti to skillet. Toss and heat.
2 tbsp./25 mL pure virgin olive oil freshly ground black pepper 4-6 sprigs of fresh basil	*Put ziti on a warm serving platter or warm plates. Drizzle with pure virgin olive oil. Sprinkle with freshly ground black pepper. Garnish with sprigs of fresh basil and serve.*

 # iti Tirrenia

Ziti with Squid and Sundried Tomatoes

Serves 4-6

Cook 1 lb./500 g ziti al dente: 3-5 minutes for fresh ziti; 5-7 minutes for packaged ziti (to cook pasta, see p. 15).

1 lb./500 g squid salt freshly ground black pepper juice of 1 lemon 2 tbsp./2 mL unsalted butter 2 tbsp./25 mL olive oil	*Clean squid by pulling off the head and pulling out the entrails. Lay squid on a cutting board or flat surface and, using a sharp knife, scrape the skin off. Wash squid thoroughly in cold running water. Cut off tentacles and make sure that the beak-like mouth is discarded. Chop tentacles and body in 1/2 inch/1 cm pieces. Pat squid dry with a cloth or paper towel. Season squid with salt, pepper and lemon juice. Sauté squid in butter and olive oil in a skillet for 2-3 minutes until golden.*
3 medium cloves garlic, finely chopped 1/2 cup/125 mL sundried tomatoes, sliced 4 tbsp./60 mL capers, drained 1/4 cup/50 mL chicken consommé (see p. 21)	*Add garlic, sundried tomatoes, capers and chicken consommé to skillet and sauté for approximately 2 minutes.*
salt freshly ground black pepper juice of 1/2 lemon	*Season with salt, pepper and lemon juice.*
	Add ziti to skillet. Toss and heat.
2 tbsp./25 mL fresh parsley, finely chopped	*Put ziti on a warm serving platter or warm plates. Sprinkle with chopped fresh parsley and serve. Cheese not recommended.*

Definition of Cooking Terms

Blanch—to scald very quickly in boiling water.
Concassé—to finely chop, unequally, in squares or cubes.
Julienne—to cut in thin strips.
Zest—the peel of a lemon.

Index

cknowledgements

Thank you to the following for the loan of props for the photography: Mrs. Dilys Maddin of Quadra Stone Company Ltd. for the loan of the marble; Umberto's Restaurants Ltd. (Il Giardino and La Cantina) for the loan of the Italian handpainted ceramic plates; The Salt Box for the loan of the red serving platter, the brown ceramic casserole dish and the large skillet; Birks and Roomers for the loan of cutlery; The Other Place (Park Royal) and The Salt Box for the loan of serviettes; Daniel Herbs for the boxes of fresh herbs; The Salt Box and Basic Stock Cookware (Patrice Taylor and Cathy Slota) for the loan of kitchen stuff; and for props loaned, but not used, W.H. Puddifoot (Olive Herendy and Mary Barnsley)—*thanks.*

This book was written in the kitchens of Il Giardino (Vancouver) and Umberto's (San Francisco) in the summer of 1984 with the assistance of Ron Lammie and Patrizio Sacchetto; it was revised in the fall of 1984 on the fly and at the *maestro's* bedside (while watching rock videos and staring at the exercise machine). Ron Lammie would like to thank Greg Van Heirden for his assistance; Patrizio Sacchetto would like to thank Raphael Lazzati and Stephen Maxwell for their assistance.

Umberto Menghi would like to thank John Bishop for his invaluable assistance, *as always;* and Marian Babchuk, *as ever.* Thanks also to Carlos Mas in San Francisco; Jöel Thibault in Seattle; and Osvaldo Fabbro, Eustacio "Chico" Tejedor and José Jorge O. Bicho in Vancouver. And thank you, Ian Robertson at Umbertino's.

David Robinson would like to thank Zonda Nellis and Michael Burch (once again); the staff at Hemlock Printers Ltd., particularly Dick and John Kouwenhoven, Wendy Smythe, Lou Mazza and Amanda Soon in typesetting, Bob McGannon and Jo Steinicke in production, and Joe Hicik and Joe Kandrack on the press; Sammy Lalji and Doug Leask at Bryan Adams' favourite restaurant, Umberto's (which is world class) for always taking care; and Derik Murray and his staff, Rob Scott, Perry Zavitz, Steve Tate and Joanne Parker—it sure was fun, guys!

And thank you, Mamma Delia. And thank you, John.